ROMANTIC CEYLON

ROMANTIC CEYLON

ITS HISTORY, LEGEND AND STORY

R. H. BASSETT

DRAWINGS BY
KATHLEEN MURDOCH
E. J. LAWS

GYAN

Published by

Gyan Publishing House
5, Ansari Road
Daryaganj, New Delhi-110002
Phone: 011-47034999, 9811692060
E-mail: books@gyanbooks.com

Distribution Network
gyanbooks.com
India, USA, Canada, UK, Australia, France

ISBN : 978-81-212-3967-7 (PB)
First Published, Colombo

2nd Impression 2020

Printed at: Gyan Press, Delhi.

Romantic Ceylon
Author: R. H. Bassett

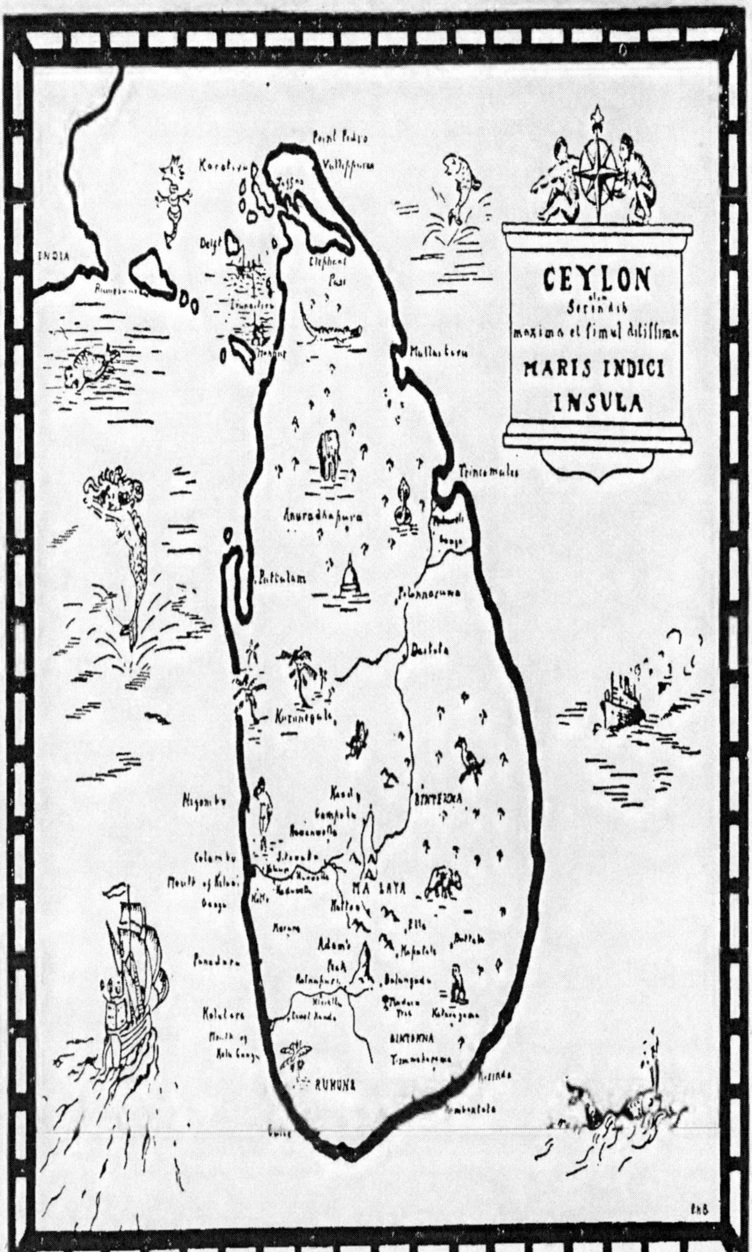

CEYLON
MARIS INDICI
INSULA
Point Pedro
INDIA
Delft
Mullaitivu
Trincomalee
Anuradhapura
Puttalam
Polonnaruwa
Kurunegala
Negombo
Kandy
Gampola
BINTENNA
Colombo
Mouth of Kelani Ganga
MALAYA
Hatton
Ella
Adam's Peak
Badulla
Kalutara
Balangoda
Kataragama
RUHUNA
Galle
Hambantota
Kirinda

ROLLING ROUND THE TEMPLE AT MAVIDDAPPURAM [Frontispiece

INTRODUCTION

LIKE the *Mahavansa*, an ancient Sinhalese chronicle, this book is written "for the supreme joy and emotion" of its readers. Intended purely to interest and amuse, it lays no claim to historical completeness or scientific method, the selection of the incidents which form its contents being governed primarily by the accident of the localities in Ceylon where the Author has worked. Each chapter endeavours to illustrate one of the myriad tags which form the huge variegated patchwork of Ceylon history and legend, but, apart from the chronological grouping of events connected with separate districts, a stereotyped system of construction has been avoided. The variety of interest thus ensured serves to emphasize the fact that the whole of Ceylon is a vast storehouse of legend and folklore, wherefrom a negligible proportion of material has been drawn to fill the following pages, not omitting the oldest stories, because they are usually the best, but also, it is hoped, including a number of tales which to most readers, at least, will be new.

The Author is indebted to the numerous people, of all races, classes and creeds, who have willingly "told the tale" to an inquisitive wanderer, and especially to Mr. Reimers, Government archivist, for the loan of his old books; while opportunity is taken to acknowledge with gratitude the generous permission granted by *The Times of Ceylon* to reproduce the articles and illustrations which form the entire contents of the book, with the exception of a few portions, for which thanks are due to the following quarters: to *The Ceylon Observer* Christmas number, for the reproduction of "Sousinha" and the story of how the King of Kandy fell into the lake; to *The Ceylon Observer Sunday Illustrated*, for the tale of Galegama Arachchi; to *The Ceylon Independent*, for "The Rice Pounder"; and to the Sport and General Press Agency, for the Frontispiece, which previously appeared in *The Sphere*.

The reader will find a Glossary on page 313, preceded by a brief List of Dates on page 311, providing an historical formula into which new factors can be fitted as desired.

CONTENTS

ILLUSTRATIONS AND MAPS

ROMANTIC CEYLON

CHAPTER ONE

CEYLON AND ITS PEOPLE

IN its conglomeration of individual races living amicably together Ceylon has a great feature in common with ancient Rome, where as long as a man was a Roman citizen he was no alien. Sinhalese, Tamil, European and Malay mingle indiscriminately in this island, like the wives of the gentleman who, having outlived all his matrimonial partners, gathered their remains into one last resting-place. Unfortunately in transport the relics became mixed, so the husband put an epitaph above them, extolling the virtues of all four, beginning with Amelia:

> "Who got mixed up together, in a wonderful manner,
> With portions of Mary and Martha and Hannah."

This ethnological anecdote admirably illustrates the commendable unity of the Ceylon nationalities, known collectively as "Ceylonese," whose virtues it is now proposed to extol.

Before dealing with conquerors and settlers, a word is necessary about the aboriginal inhabitants, called in ancient literature "Yakkhas" and "Rakshas," or devils, but usually identified at the present time with the Veddahs, who still exist in very small numbers. Just as the stage-coach is indebted to Dickens for its romantic popularity, so the Veddahs have to thank Dr. R. L. Spittel for introducing them in so attractive a fashion to the public that interest in their doings never flags. There are three sorts of these obscure people: village Veddahs, who have given up their forest life for the more social career of a Sinhalese villager; coast Veddahs, who have taken to a life of fishing round the seashore; and Veddahs without qualifications—the original genuine article—who live in the jungle, upon whatever food they can find. Beware of imitations, since in the absence of a Registered Trade Mark the impersonation of "Veddahs from the Bintenna" is practised wherever and whenever profit is to be found in it. The reputation as a hunting race that this people has acquired, though true enough, does not cover the habitual pursuit of big game; no doubt if an injured elephant is tracked his end is hastened, but the usual bag consists of mice and such small fry. The real Veddah, talking his own language, knowing no Sinhalese or Tamil, is now very scarce, due to advancing civilization, which offers inducements so infinitely more comfortable than a houseless

YOUNG CEYLON

existence of want in the wet jungle, that the numbers of those who prefer the wild life is steadily decreasing. The Wanniyas, who live on the northern edge of the North-Central Province, claim an exclusive pedigree for themselves, denying any connection with the Veddahs whom they regard as their inferiors, although in habits they are identical.

The Sinhalese are descended, through the gallant Wijaya, from an extremely beautiful but somewhat undiscriminating young lady who married a lion. This fact, which is recorded in the *Rajawaliya*, an historical volume of great age, will not be discussed here—"*Chacun a son gout.*" Wijaya himself, whose career will be found fully recorded in Chapter Three, came from Bengal, in the year 543 B.C., banished by his father for the numerous offences that he had committed against public tranquillity, along with his seven hundred companions, who were all born on the same date as himself, the day of the death of Buddha. Wijaya, after subduing the *yakkhas*, founded the present Sinhalese race. In course of time those who lived round the sea-coast have been brought under the rule of successive conquerors—Portuguese, Dutch and British—each of whom have left a distinctive trace upon the original stock, either in language, habit or appearance. Those now known as Kandyans, who spread to the hill-country—where, in the mountain fastnesses, they remained more or less immune from invasion—do not display imported characteristics to any great extent. This national division of the community is in no way connected with the social distinctions of caste, a legacy from the times when everyone had his duties about the Court, which his descendants were hereditarily bound to continue. A friendly, lively, hospitable race, ardently devoted to sport, from the lowest to the highest, the Sinhalese display one particularly estimable trait in their character: they never work unless it is absolutely necessary to do so. Most people claim to practise this doctrine, but when one has watched a Sinhalese villager putting the theory into execution one realizes how utterly incompetent are one's own efforts to fulfil the ideal.

During the third century B.C., an Indian invasion of Ceylon occurred, when the Tamils swept down upon the north of the island, laying waste the Sinhalese civilization with ruthless fire and sword. Eventually the Sinhalese stemmed the tide, and drove back the Tamil wave, until a natural limit of occupation was evolved from the constant warfare, leaving the newcomers in possession of the northern portion of the island, whence their invasion had been launched. The two races mentally and physically are very different, although both have the ready good-fellowship that distinguishes the Ceylonese; the Jaffnese, or Tamils of the north, are often referred to as the "Scotsmen of the East," on account of their business ability.

Jaffna is rather sandy, but every inch of the soil, by skilful irrigation, is made to carry a fertile crop.

The next invaders were the Portuguese, to whom single blessedness did not appeal, and whose policy of colonization by the marriage of their soldiery to the inhabitants of the conquered territory impressed a particularly indelible mark of their passage. Comparatively few Sinhalese of the Maritime Provinces have not at least one Portuguese name, while the language abounds in words such as "*almira*" (cupboard), "*kalisam*" (trousers), "*pintura*" (picture). The trimly cut goatee beard of the Conquistador is still universally in evidence, where, in his day, the swaggering Senhor set the fashion among Ceylon's youthful gallants who fought both for and against him. Either by cleverness or duplicity individual Portuguese penetrated occasionally even into the strongholds of the Kandyans. Such a one was Gascoigne, who, in the course of his service under the King of Kandy, rose to the rank of Prime Minister. Being extremely handsome, of fine stature, and withal gallant and polished of manner, it was not long before the Queen noticed him, with an attention which savoured more of affection than circumspection.

The King was jealous and suspicious, but unable to check the progress of the flirtation until he had definite proof that Gascoigne was going beyond the bounds of courtesy, such as is

"WHO TOLD YOU TO PUT THAT MOLE THERE?"

due from a Minister to his Queen. Suddenly both King and Minister were stricken by a common sorrow—the Queen fell seriously ill.

So dangerous did her condition become that a dancer had to be summoned to perform the Bali ceremony. This rite consists in dancing to the beat of tom-toms incessantly night and day, around a replica of the patient made of clay, until the sufferer dies or shows signs of recovery. The more the modelled figure resembles the original the greater the chances of a successful cure.

Before the model was completed Gascoigne sorrowfully entered the chamber where the Bali dancer was at work, to see that the task was progressing satisfactorily. Immersed in grief, for the Queen was in a critical state, the Portuguese gazed at the clay figure, anxious that it should bear the best possible resemblance to the Royal lady.

"It is good," he murmured, "quite good; but do not omit the mole above the left knee."

The dancer amended his omission.

Just then the King came in to see that the ceremony was being properly performed. Observing the mole, he said: "Dancer, who told you to put that mole there?"

"Sire," replied the dancer, "it was My Lord the Prime Minister."

Next day poor Gascoigne was beheaded. The Queen recovered. How she explained matters to the King history does not record.

There are still Portuguese in the island who talk an Orientalized Latin tongue that is rapidly dying out through lack of use. English children who have spent their youthful careers in Jaffna will have memories of "Portuguese Eliza," or "Old Mary," who directed their infant footsteps with quaint old-fashioned admonitions, and amused their tender ears with forgotten stories of fairies and animals. Mothers, too, will recollect nurse's explanation of how her young charge got into mischief: "Oh, lady, little missie running, running too fast, I old woman, not able to stop and catch."

After the Portuguese had held the coasts of Ceylon for some one hundred and thirty years they gave place to the Dutch, whose descendants, the Dutch burghers, preserving a dignity apart, pride themselves justly upon their ancestry, who ousted the Portuguese from the island. Among the numerous domestic virtues which grace the burgher ladies, the foremost is their cooking—a dream of culinary succulence.

The British entered the island in A.D. 1795, almost without violence, owing to the evacuation of the Dutch. Since that date the European community has steadily grown, especially in Colombo; it consists entirely of planters, merchants and Government servants, among all of whom, it is said, Scotsmen predominate. In a separate class may be grouped passengers. These last, although presumed to have individual national characteristics, are all of one unmistakable pattern to the lay eye, owing to the enveloping nature of their topis, and the disguising influence of warm suiting, but there is evidence to show that rickshaw coolies, guides, and other experts, are able to distinguish numerous definite species.

Besides these successive conquerors several other races, chiefly from Southern India, have been peacefully settling in Ceylon throughout the centuries. The Mukwars, who are to be found in the Puttalam and Batticaloa districts, are the descendants of a people from Malabar, who fled to the Tamil part of Ceylon rather than accept the Koran, which the conquering Arabs tried to force upon them in their own country, although, strange to say, many of them are now Mohammedans. There are also a few villages in the North-Central and North-Western Provinces where "Waga-men" live, in a separate Tamil-speaking community, descended from the captives whom King Gaju Bahu brought home with him from his South Indian wars.

It is suggested that the Kinneras—a people who are placed last in the list of castes, even below the Rodiyas—came from the Malayalam coast of India; but they know no language except Sinhalese, nor have they any tradition to that effect, although their short curly hair seems to indicate a different source of origin from the other inhabitants of the Kandyan districts. The Malayalam, who is frequently found in the capacity of bungalow servant, is a visitor from the coast of India which bears that name: he seldom becomes a permanent resident, usually returning at length to his native land, when his activities in the chicken and vegetable market have amassed for him a sufficient fortune to warrant retirement. Closely allied to the Malayalams are the Kochis, who specialize in gardeners' work. Many of them wear their hair in a picturesque knot at the side of the head—a fashion which constitutes the badge of bachelorhood, as well as giving the wearer a distinctive appearance.

Within the environs of all large towns can be met the Natukottai Chetties—a community exclusively composed of merchants, who contribute no little to the amiability of the island. They are all rich men, stout, genial, jolly fellows, whose generosity is proverbial and bluff Pickwickian manner infectious. Their success, which is carried well in front, and customarily uncovered, is both impressive and commendable.

While contemplating the Tamil nationalities, Ramasamy and Muttachchi, the modern Indian invaders must not be forgotten, with their large families of children and goats. The immigrant Indian estate labourer is a childlike soul, contented with little and easily swayed by popular rumour. He has an exceeding fondness for squatting, talking to his relations, either on the highroad or as near to the wheel tracks as is possible without being run over. His womenkind, affectionately known when young as "*kutties*" ("u" as in "put"), are frequently comely, and all possess wonderful figures. As they grow older their tongues appear to grow longer, and their voices more shrill, so that a Tamil mother-in-law is even more notorious than an English one. Offshoots from the main Tamil stream take up bungalow work, graduating from the "Podian" stage, through the "Second Servant" era, until they arrive at the goal of "Experienced Head *Appu*," whose duties are to meet visitors, see that the other servants do their work, and collect a fat "*santosum*" (tip) from departing guests.

The Moors of Ceylon—as distinct from coast Moors, who are merely Indian visitors—are said to be the descendants of Arabs driven out of Arabia in the eighth century A.D. by religious persecution. It is possible that a colony was formed in Ceylon by such immigrants, but the coming of the Arab was not an isolated incident, rather it was the slow settlement through the ages of "Mariners" (as the Sinhalese still call the Moors) along the coasts of the countries where they traded. The Ceylon Moor has now penetrated inland, where he lives in small colonies among the Sinhalese, while the coast Moor carries on the peaceful infiltration by which the race has established itself in all parts of the East. They are a quiet, cheerful, businesslike race, with the self-endorsed ambition of being left in peace to carry on their transactions. Their pleasures are simple, consisting of an occasional jaunt, tightly packed into a large motor-car, on the Hajji festival, or at some other holiday season.

The Ceylon Malays have their headquarters at Hambantota, where in ancient days they used to call in for water on their way from Malay proper to Madagascar. After a time this little port of call turned into a large settlement, increased later by the arrival of political exiles from Java. The Malay is essentially a practical man, with a liking for police work, in which capacity he spreads all over the island, retiring eventually to the old home among the sandhills of the southern coast. Robert Percival, Esq., of His Majesty's 19th Regiment, in his book on Ceylon, written in 1803, remarks with appreciation that the Malays who were serving in the Dutch army were the only troops who resisted the British entry into Colombo.

Mention of the Malays—who owe their presence in the island largely to the Dutch need for military mercenaries—leads to the consideration of the Kaffir race, now almost extinct in Ceylon, whose importation was entirely due to a similar British necessity. Until it was disbanded, the British maintained a Kaffir regiment in Colombo; but, although many of the ex-soldiers married and settled in the island, there is now little trace of them, except in the police force, which absorbed a large number of the disbanded personnel. Their famous dance, the "Kaffirina," is still performed, with increasing inaccuracy of technique, and occasionally a gentleman whose hair denotes his ancestry can be prevailed upon to sing the remnants of a national song, but the generation of Sinhalese now growing up expresses surprise on hearing that there ever were Kaffirs in Ceylon.

A picturesque figure takes the final place upon the stage: the Afghan, who, upon note of hand alone, will generously fork out, to those who are hard up, at a surprising rate of interest. It is difficult to see how he makes his fortune, since he appears to find it hard to get the money back again, in spite of his commanding presence. After pay-day he can be observed patiently standing round the office doors in the fort, waiting for the clerk—who has climbed out of a window at the other side of the house. He has a racial characteristic when in Ceylon which is unique, and apparently obscure in its origin—namely, his habit of wearing stout army-pattern boots. Where he gets them is at present an unanswered question. It would, of course, be possible to ask an Afghan, but, besides being contrary to the rules of controversy ever to solve the problem at issue, the wearer of the boots would probably put one off with a non-committal answer, or even hit one over the head with the large stick which he invariably carries. At the time of the Hajji festival it is a very impressive sight to see all the Afghans gathered together on the Galle Face, where, in two ranks, they conduct their worship collectively, led by a senior who gives the time for the various evolutions, kneeling in front of his fellow-worshippers for that purpose.

These are the races of Ceylon separately considered. Naturally, with so many divergent interests, it is not often that they can be observed collectively as "Ceylonese," but sport, the leveller, gives that opportunity. During the August Week Races, in the humble one-rupee enclosure of the race-course, every nationality is represented among the huge crowd which gathers with the common object of trying to get something for nothing by sporting means.

The most striking feature of the one-rupee enclosure is dust; not intolerably thick, but warm, brown, and slightly smelly. The atmosphere, however, in no way detracts from the keen enjoyment depicted on the faces of the numerous patrons of the turf who frequent the less expensive parts of the race-course. Among these enthusiasts, members of all classes of "*dukpat minisu*" (poor men) mingle in happy familiarity, oblivious of caste or religion. Respectable elderly ladies urge their young nephews to put a rupee on the favourite for them at the totalizator, in just the same way as their wealthier counterparts across the course compel the services of elegant, but secretly reluctant, young men for the same purpose. "*Aiyo*, the aunt wants her money on a horse that will win . . . One on Jorn Clunshie, Mahatmaya. . . How little she will get if it wins did you say? . . . Yes, but how little I shall get when the old woman dies if I put her money on any more horses that lose this afternoon."

The Tamil coolie takes a ticket at every sweepstake booth, and has a rupee on at the "tote" as well—on the assumption that the more you put down the more you may pick up. Then, after an interminable argument with his friends, about which ticket belongs to which place, eventually he presents his "tote" coupon to a sweep official, who abruptly calls him a fool, without telling him why, thereby leaving him more mystified than before. There are, however, plenty of willing helpers for one in the coolie's predicament. If the ticket owner is large and suspicious they will undertake to unravel the problem for a small fee, but if he is of little account they take his ticket to the booth for nothing, on the chance of drawing the money for a win and telling the legitimate winner that he drew a blank.

In the coterie of junior clerks the technicalities of racing are discussed with knowledgeable familiarity. "Steven, I say, what will win at the 3·30?" "My heart tells me Dalkester will come first." "What, with such weight; he has been loaded so heavily, how can he prevail?"

Two dignified elderly Mohammedans meet for the first time since the last day's racing; with restrained joy they gaze at one another for a moment, each with a hand on the shoulder of his friend, while the essential questions are asked: "How is the father? And the mother? And all the relations?" Then, if all are well, the important query of the day is broached: "What is going to win the Guvnar Iscup?"

"The start is made," shouts an excited punter.

"Sitting here shall I be safe?" asks an old lady, who feels rather flustered by the crowd. "From the horses, yes, Amma, but from the men, never," replies a young wit—by whose retort Amma, despite the laughter, is decidedly flattered.

"Look, Soysa is in front, he will win, I said he would."

"Let me see, Tamby. I have ticket for him."

"Who's pushing? Get off my foot, then I can move."

"*Aiyo*, see my horse, he is coming last. He has the stomach-ache, or else they have given him no food."

"Here they come, Soysa. Soysa-a-a-a-a! He's won. He's first. I will get my money and come."

The purr of cars coming down the course announces the arrival of His Excellency, an episode that concentrates attention for a time on the Grand Stand. "That's the Guvnar, in the middle of the big house, above the flowers," remarks someone.

"No, it is not—you do not know anything, Cornelis; it is Darbegum" (Sir Herbert Dowbiggin, Inspector-General of Police).

"You may be right, Andiris, you know the polis well."

This interchange of repartee leads to a short round of abuse, which is terminated by the interference of a stout elderly Sinhalese, who relates impressively how he once lost two thousand rupees, which were recovered for him by the personal exertions of the I.G.P. No one believes him, but the story serves to distract the thoughts of the disputants long enough for their tempers to cool.

From the centre of the course the race crowd makes a delightful picture in the sparkling sunlight; the foreground is filled by a dazzling array of many-hued sunshades, backed, tier upon tier, by brilliant splashes of colour, where gorgeous sarees and shining silks form a huge spangled rectangle, in the shade of the towering Grand Stand.

The absence of din and shouting is a marked feature of Colombo races, attributable mainly to the fact that there are no bookies, side-shows or tipsters—institutions which, though attractive, are inherently noisy. In spite of their comparative silence the racing public enjoys itself none the less, in the quiet manner that distinguishes a Ceylon crowd. Among the dense throng in the centre of the course a "drunk" is very exceptional, while disorderliness and fighting is neither contemplated nor tolerated. Exactly where the pleasure lies for some of the enthusiasts it is difficult to say, since their whole time is spent squatting in the dust, where the assembly is thickest, whence assuredly they never see a single race. The Sinhalese from the district, with most of his family in attendance, parades the enclosure with confidence, or glides deferentially about, according to whether he has been racing before or not, and garrulous or glum in proportion to his wins or losses. The dock labourer, often decidedly a "hard case," strolls among his friends with a genial air of independence that challenges criticism of his lack of a racing garment, while alongside the rails lounges a mercantile or Government clerk, clad in elaborately cut gentleman's suiting—whereof one Oxford-trouser leg could easily encase his entire body. One or two C.L.I. privates in uniform move about in a smart and soldierly manner, creating a profound impression upon the unsophisticated visitors. Afghans sit in contemplative groups, apparently disinterested in the proceedings, except while the actual races are being run, while small parties of students scutter past, wrangling cheerfully about the respective merits of their favourite horses.

Round the "tote" the winners press five and six deep, waving their tickets and good-humouredly badgering the Mahatmaya for their money, while others struggle to back their fancy for the next race. In the event of an objection the pressure on the front rank becomes enormous, the fortunate ones who secured places nearest the pay-desk leaning over the barrier with livid faces, as their ribs groan beneath the strain.

For the guidance of race-goers it may be observed here that on the last day of the races it is a useful tip to back what the "G.O.H." waiters call the "*pulluk aswayo*," or horses that have already run unsuccessfully in other races. "*Pulluk aswayo*" is a little-known Sinhalese term not difficult to analyse: "*aswayo*" means "horses," and "*pulluk*" is a corruption of the English words "pulled up."

In this congenial atmosphere the Ceylonese people can safely be left to enjoy themselves while attention is directed to the country of Ceylon itself, but this subject needs for its adequate appreciation the brush rather than the pen. Glittering seascapes, green domesticity of paddy-land and palm grove, rugged beauty of mountain range and crashing waterfall, limitless monotony of grey-green lowland jungle, make prose description seem almost an impertinence. On a sunny day, among the northern islands, when the fleecy clouds roll slowly across the sky, the fishing-boats lie in an opalescent mirror, framed by dazzling white beaches, above which tower black walls of palmyrah-trees, whose stately heights are reflected in the water's edge so that each island appears to stand on another upturned. Or resting at night, with the quiet splash of waves against the side of the boat, the dense gloom of the encircling tree-clothed islands is intensely impressive, when the low deep boom of a tom-tom from the great Cobra Temple on Nainativu comes rhythmically pulsating over the shimmering water. These seductive islets and blue lagoons, whose dark-shaded back-waters still afford the seclusion essential to the retiring mermaid, fascinate the imagination, but, in contrast, there is the view through the mountain cleft at Ella, where, framed by the steep sides of the valley, the vast stretch of the Bintenna jungle, with small hills rising like islands from an ocean of forest, fades in the haze of distance to a silver streak which indicates the line of the sea.

Amid such scenes as these, varying with individual beauty according to the characteristics of the landscape in each province, are set the legends and incidents which fill the following chapters.

CHAPTER TWO

BINTENNA

THE desire to see the unique—a human ambition that irresistibly stirs many people to activity—has so far inspired very few investigators to visit the only Madara tree in Ceylon. On account of its rarity this tree has commanded interest and admiration since the earliest times, when the flowers were so uncommon that they were regarded as supernatural products of heaven, worn only by angels and goddesses. Sri Rahula, in his poem *Guttila*, refers to them as follows: " He who has seen the goddesses dance to the enchanting music of violins and bells, with Madara wreaths in the soft, long tresses of their dark braided hair, adorned with strings of shining pearls like creepers to entwine the heart of the God of Love, will be content and not aspire even to be King of the Gods."

In addition to the heavenly splendour of its flowers the wood of the tree is a sure charm against the attack of elephants and a cure for the bite of snakes, while many regard it as a remedy for almost any evil or sickness. From Balangoda the journey to this marvel of the forest can be accomplished with the least discomfort, but it cannot be denied that in the dry weather the trip is excessively hot and in the wet weather objectionably wet, while, in addition to the fact that the tree grows in an exceptionally malarial district, a very long walk is necessary to reach it.

Apart from the inhabitants of the neighbourhood, the number of those who have seen this botanical rarity must be infinitesimal; certainly it does not include more than four or five Europeans now living in Ceylon. Pleasant anticipations of easy going are raised by travelling the first eight miles of the way in a car, but beyond Rajawaka the country gradually becomes wilder, until at M'olamure the last houses on the edge of the Tanjantenna plateau form a convenient halting-place.

From here the path runs through the scrub and mana-grass of Tanjantenna—a plain lying between the first foothills of the Uva mountains and the top of the cliff that falls sheer to the Bintenna jungle. In the wet weather numerous elephants climb up from the dense forests around the Walawe river, in order to escape from the elephant-flies which bother them on the lower level; while leopards are common enough to be seen beside the path at mid-day. The slight eminences that stud the plateau enclose glades of scattered trees, growing amid the tall grass, bleached white by the August sun—a type of landscape which in India would be an ideal haunt for a tiger. Looking down from the edge of the precipice on the incalculable myriads of trees, the task of finding a particular specimen seems almost impossible, but the few who know the exact position of the Madara find no difficulty in its location. As the descent from the plateau is negotiated the atmosphere becomes noticeably warmer, until at the bottom, in the thick scrub, the air is uncomfortably still and hot.

It is hard to realize that at one time this extensive wilderness was covered with prosperous towns and villages, but the innumerable ancient bricks that carpet the jungle, and the frequent mounds that indicate the sites of ruined buildings, bear irrefutable testimony to the forgotten golden age of Kongala Bintenna, when powerful chiefs held sway over the thronging cities which are now shown on the map as "ruins," amid a featureless area of "forest." The population of this district must have been immense, comparable at the present day to parts of the Western Province, where as, along the Mount Lavinia road, house jostles house in endless continuity.

At evening in the jungle it is possible to repeople this vanished kingdom with the heroes of Ruhuna who fill the pages of the *Mahavansa* with their miraculous activities. Along the street of low red-brick houses strides one of

Duttha Gamini's giants, bound upon an errand of his Royal master, contemptuous of the civilians who barter and chaffer in their shops and offices. Soldiers of the Frontier Guard lounge at the street corners, eyeing the slave-girls who pass to draw water at the municipal tank, while a palanquin passes, bearing on a visit to a friend a wealthly lady, guarded by her retinue of family retainers. Children play at the doors of their houses, and down a broad road in the dusk comes a huge elephant carrying the local chieftain to an official function. But the dark outlines of roofs and walls fade gradually into the shadowy tracery of trees and scrub, while the elephant carries no rider, but is coming down the same path to the Walawe river that has been used for centuries by his kind, since his forbears first took possession of the deserted city, when the jungle closed upon its decaying environs.

Various causes have been suggested for the eclipse of this early civilization, but it seems most probable that a combination of circumstances contributed to its downfall. The invaders from Bengal—Wijaya and his followers, who founded the Sinhalese race—used the aboriginal inhabitants as a labour force in building these cities and digging the innumerable tanks which stored water for the citizens, acting themselves as construction engineers, foremen and skilled labourers. The aborigines, however, after a time, dwindled in numbers so alarmingly, owing to absorption and extermination, that compulsory labour had to be introduced among the Sinhalese themselves. This was a less satisfactory system, in that invasion or internal strife resulted in cessation of work, since all the labourers were also fighters. Now, in the Bintenna, if irrigation ceases life stops with it; cultivation there is carried on in spite of the climate, not assisted by local conditions, so that failure to maintain the tanks, owing to the disorganization of war, resulted in disaster. Starvation followed, and malaria, which appears wherever there are neglected irrigation works, finished the havoc.

While traversing the Bintenna any sudden noise that breaks the silence of the dense scrub brings the villagers to a halt, until it has been ascertained that a herd of elephants is not concealed round the next bend of the path. In the dry weather the absence of water is very marked: stream after stream is passed without a trickle among the huge footprints in the baked mud, where elephants crossed or disported themselves before the drought began.

The geographical position of the Madara tree is no secret; on the mile-to-the-inch map of Ceylon "Two Historical Madara Trees" are shown, but without the assistance of someone who knows the location it would be next to impossible to find the exact place. The information which is usually vouchsafed to the

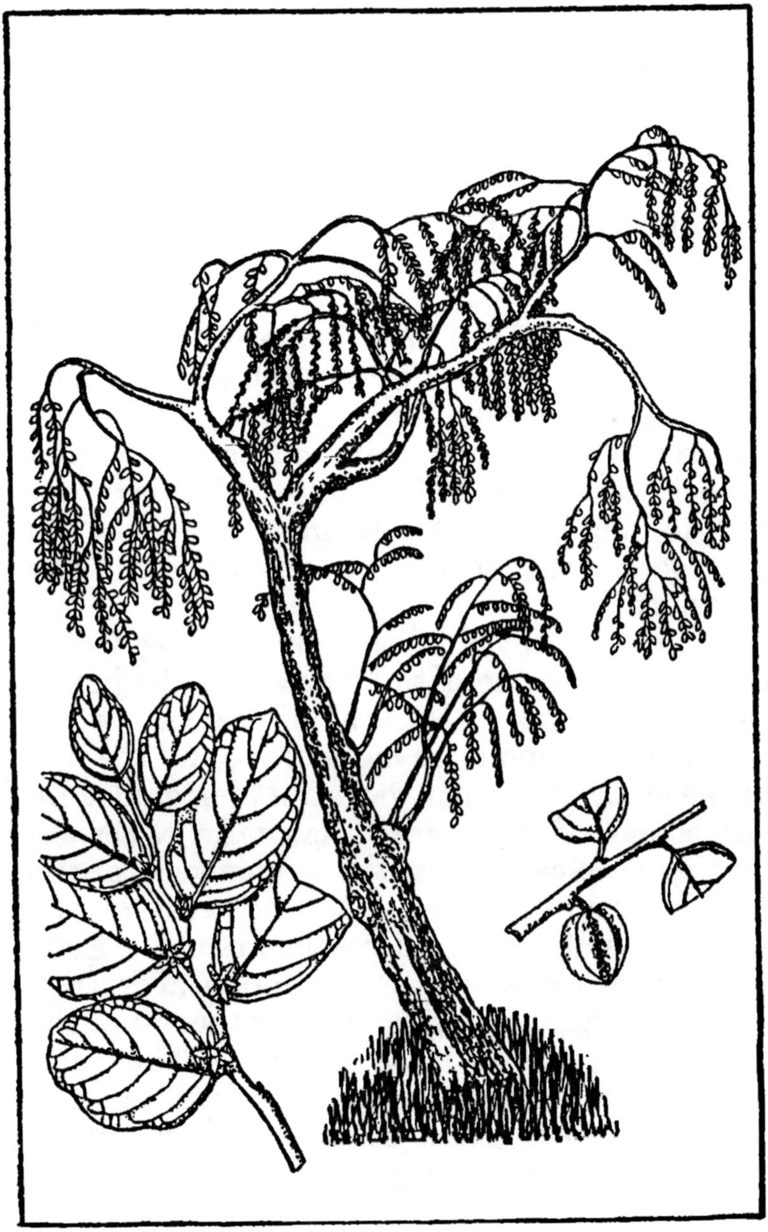

THE MADARA TREE

inquirer, that a path has been worn to the tree by the feet of pilgrims, who have removed all except the topmost branches, is incorrect; there is no approach track of any kind to indicate where to leave the Gansabhawa road and strike off into the thicket. The natural question arises as to how numerous people come to possess small pieces of the wood without leaving any trace of their passage to the tree. The answer is supplied by the villagers, who say that the hermit who lives at Kurugala, on the plateau, comes down now and then to cut a branch, which he divides into little pieces for sale to pilgrims at his shrine. Otherwise no one goes near the place, except on rare occasions.

When the leader of the party recognizes a certain spot on the path he goes into the jungle to find the tree. After a minute or two a "hoo-cry" announces his success, and the rest of the party push their way after him, guided by the sound of his voice. Naturally a certain lurking suspicion as to the genuineness of the identification remains, until the sight of the Madara itself dispels all possible doubt. Even without the aid of an accurate botanical description its unique appearance among the rest of the jungle trees marks it as a rarity. The first characteristic that strikes the eye is the amazingly fresh green of its leaves compared with the drab whitish grey of the surrounding dry-season foliage.

Considering its magic properties, the tree is not so mutilated as might be expected, although bearing numerous scars from the depredations of charm-hunters. Its alleged efficacy as a deterrent of elephants is probably attributable to the extremely poisonous character of the bark and fruit, but its protective influence is not very far-reaching, since the neighbouring trees are scarred by the marks of an elephant's tusks, thus belying the story that for many yards round the magic bole the jungle is untrodden by the feet of animals.

The following detailed description of the Madara is taken, without technicalities, from a book on Indian forestry, supplemented by notes made at the tree itself.

Its Latin name is *Cleistanthus collinus*, and it belongs to the order *Euphorbiaci*. It is a small tree, about the size of an average apple-tree, with stout, crooked, spreading branches that tend to grow downwards at the ends. The bark of the trunk and old branches is dark grey and black; it is exceedingly rough and scaly, being split up all over its surface into small concave pieces, irregular as to size and outline. The young branches are so completely different as to make them look as if they belonged to another tree. Their bark is soft and corky, with a surface intensely roughened by innumerable longitudinal crevices; the colour is greyish yellow with a tinge of red, overlaid by a whitish bloom, which disappears when the stick is held long in the hand. The mature timber is dark reddish brown, very hard indeed, and gives off a pungent aroma when cut; but the young wood is yellowish white, without smell. The twigs are hairy and very sticky to touch, a feature that indicates the poisonous character of the bark and fruit.

The leaves are few, and of a bright, light green colour on the upper surface, with paler green under sides; they hang vertically, point downwards, upon very short stalks, on alternate sides of the twig, at one-and-a-half-inch intervals, lessening to one inch near the extremity of the spray. The larger leaves near the base of the twig are about four inches long, decreasing in size to some two inches at the farther end. They hang back to back, each just overlapping its neighbour on either side, looking, with their oval shape and blunt points, like a row of little flat fish hanging on a stick or string. The veining of the leaves is netlike or reticulate. Clusters of yellow, small-petalled flowers appear in May, each blossom springing from a hairy cup or calyx, which is composed of minute portions, shaped like lance-heads, and called sepals. A smooth, woody, brown fruit follows the flower; it is indistinctly three-lobed, and roughly three-quarters of an inch in diameter, containing almost spherical seeds with six plainly marked divisions. It is a singular fact that, although several people have possessed seeds of the Ceylon tree, no one has succeeded in making one grow, while a seed picked up below the tree, where it had lain for three months, showed no sign of any effort to sprout. As is indicated by the map, the present tree had at one time a companion, which died of old age and was removed, while a third specimen in another district, called Kolonna, if local information is to be believed, suffered the same fate. In India the Madara occurs in the Satpura range, and is very common in Oudh, whence seeds have lately been obtained for experimental growth in Ceylon, without success.

The walk along the bank of the Walawe to Uggal-Kaltota Irrigation Bungalow is brimming with jungle interest, especially in the evening, when the words of a famous song, "*Down in the Forest something stirred,*" assume their fullest import, as an ominous crashing of bushes near the path announces the stirring of something undesirably large. Armed with a piece of Madara there is, of course, nothing to fear, but it is advisable for the traveller to be near a climbable tree when a wild buffalo crosses the path, leaving the Walawe after his bathe.

There is an appropriate "*kemma*" (charm) against every evil; but the verse that helps to keep away elephants is too complicated to remember, and apparently has no meaning; in fact the theory is advanced, by one who has studied the problem very exhaustively, that the purpose of the sounds is rather like wireless telegraphy, to create a series of atmospheric vibrations which, in this case being distasteful to the elephant, irritate his ear-drums and so instigate him to go away from their unpleasant influence as soon as he can.

The preventive action against jungle-ticks is, however, rather practical than verbal, besides being both effective and simple. If possible, without being observed, pluck a spray of leaves off any bush, with the right hand, from behind you as you pass; then, without mentioning the action, or displaying the least consciousness of doing anything unusual, stick the twigs in the top of the shorts or cloth at the back. After this precaution has been taken ticks can be treated with contempt, they will not trouble the wearer of the *kemma.* It is better, although not essential, to be unobserved when affixing the leaves, but a remark about the action, or the betrayal of the least self-consciousness in its execution, is fatal to the efficacy of the charm. As an example of the necessity for observing these rules an authentic instance can be quoted, when sixteen ticks were removed from the person of a policeman who had made a frivolous joke about his *kemma.* This circumstance, as well as emphasizing the importance of correct procedure in the conduct of magic exercises, also shows the fearlessness of the tick. When the *kemma* is removed it should be held in the right hand and passed with a stroking motion, first down the right side of the body, from head to foot, then down the left, after which it must be crumpled up and thrown away. These last motions remove any ticks that may have penetrated its protective influence.

It is inauspicious to speak of a dangerous animal by its usual name when in the jungle, lest the mere mention of the creature should precipitate the coincidence of an immediate encounter with it. Hence the elephant is spoken of as "*maha bola*" ("the big ball"); the leopard as "*mutta*" ("great-grandfather"); while in Sabaragamuwa the bear is known as "Soma," a girl's name, and in Uva as "*as-vedda*" ("the eye-doctor"), because of his habit of attacking his victim's eyes or face.

At Budugala, where the path joins the irrigation channel serving Uggal-Kaltota paddy-fields, are some very ancient ruins, said to be those of a "*dewale*" (temple), connected with Uggal Alutnuwara Dewale, near Balangoda, which owns a field in the Kaltota "*yaya*" (stretch of cultivation). From here there is a splendid view of the massive Kurugala rock, towering in bleak magnificence above the low country. This aspect of the cliff has an added interest, in that a dark patch of vegetation growing about half-way up the face of the precipice is said to be a bush of the famous Kalu Nika, whose twig brings good health and good fortune. It is quite inaccessible, a characteristic of the tree that renders it a great rarity, not to be compared with the Madara in that respect, but sufficiently uncommon to attract numerous legends about its magic properties. Whenever the "*atikukula*" (skinny-chicken), or jungle "crow," is able to find a stick of this tree, it builds it into its nest, knowing full well its value as a charm against evil influences. Anyone who discovers a jungle "crow's" nest is thus afforded an opportunity to acquire a piece of Kalu Nika, but it is a laborious business to find it amongst the mass of sticks of which the big dome-shaped structure is composed. Twig by twig the nest should be thrown into a running stream, or into a fire, until a piece is observed to float upstream, or to resist the disintegrating effect of the flames. That will be the Kalu Nika. Such is its power that, if a young jungle "crow" is put in a cage, the parent bird will search the forest until it finds a piece to place on the youngster's prison. Immediately the Kalu Nika touches the cage the latter collapses and the little one escapes. The veracity of this phenomenon might be tested by experiment before it is accepted as a natural historical fact.

Along the whole length of the five-mile channel that feeds eight hundred acres of paddy-fields the path forms a delightfully pretty and shady walk at any time of day. In the thick jungle which grows down to the water's edge deer can frequently be seen drinking, and the call of the jungle fowl is constantly heard, while monkeys play in the fern-covered trees, whose branches they share with the big rock-squirrel.

The "*ehela*" (laburnum), with its delicate clusters of yellow flowers, displays splashes of bright colour among the dark greens and browns of the forest, which on the channel banks is unscorched by drought, shading flowers that a few yards away would shrivel in the baked earth. Among the plants which flourish along the margin of this stream is the Gurullu-rajah; it grows to a height of two feet, bearing a pink flower, succeeded by an oval seed with two horns at its tip that are said to resemble the proboscis of a kind of bluish wasp, called the *gurullaya.* The seed is also known as the "*naga-darana*" (curled cobra), because it is not unlike the raised head of that snake. Herein lies perhaps the root of its magic properties, which make it much sought after by the *chetty* community as a charm against evil. The seed presents a double illusion: it looks like a cobra's head, but the little projections also make it resemble the snake's mortal enemy, the *gurullaya,* who, whenever opportunity offers, kills the cobra by settling upon its head and stinging it through to the brain.

The modern irrigation channel was reconstructed by Mr. Wace and Mr. Fred Lewis, along the trace of a very ancient watercourse that is said to have extended at one time as far as Diyainna—a distance of sixteen miles. Mr. Wace, who was Government Agent in this district for eleven years, is still remembered with unabated affection as the "Kotiya-Eganta" ("the

Tiger Agent"), a nickname he acquired from his habit of shouting when annoyed. Not only is his memory green in the recollection of those who knew him, but he has become a tradition which is handed on to generations that knew him not, such was the respect and liking that his character inspired among the villagers.

The original channel was made by a giant named Nila Maha Yodaya, who, in the dawn of history, selected the barren district of Kaltota for the purpose of a vast irrigation scheme. Choosing two rocks near the present *anicut*, he cut sockets in them, which can still be seen, and affixed therein huge beams to form a dam across the Walawe, known as the Yodaya *bemma*. His principal difficulty was, however, to decide in what direction to dig the channel that would carry the water to his proposed fields. He solved this problem with immense acumen. Noticing an "*uk*" (sugar-cane leaf), of which one end was caught in some rocks, streaming out in the water like a pennon, and correctly deducing from this observation the set of the current, he dug his channel in the direction indicated by the leaf, with such success that the trace is still in use.

It was a complicated circumstantial chain which led to the arrival at this position of the leaf, whose portentous influence conferred upon Kaltota the prefix Uggal. The *uk* became detached from its parent sugar-cane in the Uggal Dova—a valley above Belihul Oya, just below the Horton Plains, where a tea estate has succeeded an old coffee venture. The original Kovila, or Temple of the God Kataragama Kandasamy, where his "*hellaya*" (lance) was kept, stood here, on the site, so it is said, of the modern estate bungalow; but it was moved in the course of years to Alutnuwara Dewale, near Balangoda, which subsequently, for that reason, was called Uggal Alutnuwara. Falling into the Hiri Katti Oya, the leaf floated down that stream into the Belihul Oya, and thence to the Walawe, where it drifted until, becoming entangled in the rocks at Kaltota, it delivered its silent message of enlightenment to the Nila Maha Yodaya.

As soon as the channel was cut, the giant set to work with immense energy and cultivated thirty-five *yalas* of paddy-land on each side of the Walawe, boasting that at the end of the harvest he would make a pile of paddy so high that the sea would be visible from its summit. After his first reaping he threshed the rice and piled it all in one huge heap, telling his son to climb to the top and say if he could see the sea. Now the giant's wife was a greedy and avaricious woman. As her son started the ascent, she whispered to him to say that he could not see the sea, whether he saw it or not, so that her husband would cultivate even more land next year, in order to fulfil his boast, and so they would become very rich. Listening to his mother's bad advice, although he clearly saw the sun shining on the sea, he said that he could not see it; but his lie had an effect opposite to that which the giant's wife had desired. Disgruntled, because he thought his harvest was not so great as he had predicted, the Nila Maha Yodaya scattered the paddy to the winds, kicked down the dam across the Walawe, and went away, never to return. For centuries the Kaltota fields lay waste, but at length, on the Sabaragamuwa side of the river, the land was again brought under cultivation, until now a harvest is reaped from eight hundred acres, but on the Uva bank of the Walawe the fields are abandoned to the jungle for lack of water—a situation which will continue until another irrigation giant rebuilds the dam.

Among places in Ceylon with a bad reputation for fever Uggal Kaltota can claim to be in the first rank. The inhabitants are fully aware that it is the mosquito which spreads the disease, but these insects swarm in such myriads that the people are powerless to avoid them, with the result that very few, if any, of them go through the year without at least one bad attack of malaria. "Katol" sticks are effective at night, in the closely sealed atmosphere of the village houses, where the mosquito-killing smoke cannot escape. This fact is realized by the villagers, who welcome a fairly divided and liberal supply of this commodity more than any other gift. The hospital is a very popular institution, supplying a real need of the locality, where, as is so often the case, the complement of picturesque scenery is an extremely unhealthy climate.

Looking up the steep forest-covered cliff above Kaltota, where rock caves, and thicket provide lairs for bears and leopards, some of the thrills can be imagined which the explorers experienced in Sir Arthur Conan Doyle's book, *The Lost World.* Each turn of the ascending path holds exciting possibilities, while on peeping into a parklike glade of yellow mana-grass, from the shelter of the thick jungle belt that fringes the cliff-top, the vision of a dinosaurus drinking at a water-hole might cause alarm but, in a setting so exactly materializing the modern conception of its habitat, would occasion little surprise. After climbing the cliff to Tanjantenna's farthest limit, the traveller can look back over the country he has lately traversed, spread out below him in a mighty panorama of unbroken jungle through which a winding line of darker green indicates the course of the Walawe.

The path along the Tanjantenna plateau, especially in the dry season, is uncomfortably warm, and blessed with very little shade, but the scrub teems with animal life. Even at midday leopards play beside the track, so intent upon their game as to be oblivious for a few moments of the presence of a human being. It is said by the Sinhalese that the hornbill ("*kandatta*"), an exceedingly common bird in this district, is unable to drink owing to some physical defect, so that the poor creature is constantly thirsty, and can be seen, when it rains, sitting on a branch with its head thrown right back and its capacious beak wide open, catching the drops. It suffers from this disability as an example to all other creatures, since in former lives all hornbills have been people who refused water to the thirsty.

Four miles from Molamure there is a turn-off in the midst of "the altogether uninhabited interior," leading to Kurugala, the great cliff at the edge of the Tanjantenna plateau. Here lives a Mohammedan hermit named Mastan, whose shrine is visited annually by numbers of pilgrims. In the face of the cliff is a large cave which constitutes the scene of his devotions, although no sign of any religious significance adorns the cavern. Originally, it is said, a Mohammedan prince from India, who had committed a serious sin, decided to walk until he found a suitable place to sit and meditate upon his evil life, with the object of expiating his crime by force of concentrated contemplation. When, in the course of his wanderings, he arrived at Kurugala it struck him as the ideal for which he was looking; so he lived there for a number of years until, feeling himself redeemed, he returned to his Indian kingdom. The cave then became a Buddhist sanctuary, passing later again to the Mohammedan faith after a considerable period when no hermit lived there at all. Pilgrim bands, conducted by priests from the mosque at Balangoda, used to go to Kurugala, even when an Egyptian ex-soldier tenanted the shrine, but the present occupant, after considerable litigation, allows no other institution to interfere with his monopoly of those devout ones whose faith sustains them over the arduous journey to his cave. Before Mastan's tenancy, during the first year of the war, strange lights were reported to emanate from this retreat, supposed to have been signals transmitting to the coast messages sent from the Haputale district. When a man of unusual appearance was heard to have taken up his residence at Kurugala, investigations were made, resulting in the discovery of a very fair person, presumed to be another Egyptian by those who saw him. This individual, whose only explanation of his presence was that he liked living there, was firmly requested to leave the locality, which he did, and was not seen again.

Mastan, a hermit to whom the resources of civilization are not unknown, keeps a small path open through the jungle for the convenience of himself and his pilgrims. He does not live in the cave shrine itself, but has constructed an excellent little house in an old rock dwelling, under the eaves of an overhanging cliff adjoining Kurugala, where, with his wife and family, he lives in comfort, among poultry and pigeons, unbothered by rates and taxes. This hermit *de luxe* is a picturesque figure, with long hair, a split lip, and large, very luminous eyes; he wears a long cloak and always carries a gun in self-defence against the event of meeting a bear or wild buffalo. He has evidently not yet acquired the knack, that some saints have had, of being on familiar terms with all kinds of animals.

The cave itself is a most interesting place; it is entirely natural, bearing no signs of artificial excavation, or even of ritual adornment. The entrance is situated in the face of the cliff, a short climb down from the summit, where, on entering, there is a large "hall," from which two passages lead off on either hand. When the eyes grow used to the darkness the right-hand passage is seen to extend for at least fifty yards into the depths of the earth, before merging into the general blackness of the shadows. After following this side gallery for about thirty yards the floor is found to descend abruptly to the brink of a pit, which is said to be the mouth of an underground passage to Mecca. A virtuous soul once tested the accuracy of this legend; as he never returned from his investigations it can be assumed that he found the story to be true. Mastan crosses the abyss on a thin tree trunk, by the light of a match, but the average visitor will be content to let his explorations stop on the near edge of the hole. On the opposite side of the entrance hall a narrow descending passage leads out on to the "*tapas pila*" ("meditation ledge")—a niche in the sheer side of the cliff, some six feet wide and four feet broad, with an overhanging roof of rock.

Here, seated beneath the huge mass that towers fifty feet above, on the edge of a six-hundred-foot precipice, a hermit can find solitude indeed, and food for contemplation in the unbroken ocean of trees spread out below him. Entering from a small hole in the rock at the back, an atmosphere of complete detachment pervades the occupant of the tiny ledge; earthly considerations lose their importance before the uncomplicated immensity of the colossal landscape and the fatality of the sheer abyss. The inmate of a prison is far less solitary. Judging from the polish which the floor has taken, the ledge has been used for many years; certainly the Mohammedan prince was right in his choice of a suitable place wherein to expiate a crime if he lived here alone. A peculiar mark, caused by water trickling over the slightly honeycombed surface of the rock, stretches from the ceiling down the side wall of the niche, looking exactly like the cast skin of a huge snake. The presence of this damp-stain is ascribed to supernatural powers in the same way as a small roughly cut imitation of the Adam's Peak Footprint, which has been carved in a natural indentation in another smaller cave. By lying with the head over the edge of the precipice, the so-called Kalu Nika can be seen some hundred feet below. From this position the local "*arachchi*" (headman), who is rather a sceptic, says it is an "*atamuru*" (wild fig) tree, but the true identification awaits the opinion of an expert.

Back from Kurugala to Molamure the path must have been a weary walk when it was only a track marked by little heaps of stones ; but now, although blazing hot, it is easy to follow through the scrub, which here, as down below, is filled with ruins of past greatness. Near the track there stand, in the jungle, a few pillars and remnants of an ancient *vihare.* It was a building of size and importance, to which great sanctity still attaches ; so much so that it is said that when a forest fire burns the mana-grass and scrub it stops at the temple limits, burning round the outside, and joining up again behind, to leave the venerable site an oasis of green amid the blackened landscape.

CHAPTER THREE

RUHUNA

RUHUNA, although it suggests the name of a heroine in sensational fiction, is generally known to be the title applied to the southern part of Ceylon. Originally, so it is said, it was the name of an Indian prince who ruled the district shortly after the death of his uncle, the great Wijaya. The whole area covers a vast extent of territory, but it is proposed to consider in detail only the small locality between Tissamaharama and Hambantota, in which is included the ancient capital and heart of Southern Ceylon.

Except for the paddy-fields around Tissamaharama, and a small stretch of cultivated land below Wirawila, this district is a dry, arid wilderness of scrub jungle, pitted at frequent intervals with abandoned tanks and their overgrown fields—desolate ruins of past prosperity. Mr. Woolf's well-known book, *The Village in the Jungle*, written about this locality, ably describes the conditions of life of many of its inhabitants, who earn a precarious livelihood in a discouraging environment of ever-encroaching jungle.

Adhering to the formula of history, it is found that, about the year 307 B.C., the Ruhuna was described as "fertile and productive." Examination of the land shows that, until a far later period, it was a region of plenty, with a large population who exploited its resources and attended to the duties of irrigation. Normally a country of moderate rainfall, in 1780, there were stupendous downpours for a very long period, causing the tanks to overflow and breach their bunds so seriously that there was not time to repair them before the sowing season. This catastrophe resulted in a severe famine, when the population fled northward to avoid starvation. The whole irrigation system was disorganized, and although some of the tanks were repaired later, the people as a whole never came back.

Like the West of England in Danish and Roman days, the Ruhuna, in ancient times, was the last stronghold, both of the Sinhalese race and of Buddhism, against Tamil invaders. When Elara ruled the rest of Ceylon the south was yet in the hands of the Sinhalese, who at length went forth under Duttha Gamini to drive the Tamils from Anuradhapura.

All the momentous events of old time which happened in Ruhuna centre around Tissamaharama, where, on the bank of Magama river, are the ruins of a civilization contemporaneous with that of Anuradhapura. This ancient city was called Mahagama—a name that still exists in the modern village of Magama, and the stream upon which it stands, as well as in the title of the whole neighbourhood ot Magam Pattu.

At the present day Tissamaharama is a peaceful, prosperous village, whose well-being is all the more emphasized by the surrounding desolation. In the middle of the expanse of fertile paddy-fields, lying below Tissa tank, towers the restored Tissamaharama Dagoba—the whole scene an eloquent testimony to the sustained energy of modern irrigation engineering and the activity of Buddhist enthusiasm.

The repairs to this dagoba in 1883 were carried out by the same methods as those probably employed in its original construction. Leading to the scaffolding on which the bricklayers worked a bamboo ladder was erected, on each rung of which stood a builder, who received a brick from the man below him and handed it to the man above. It was suggested that a winch at the foot of the dagoba would facilitate matters, but the builders, all of whom were working voluntarily, would not hear of such a suggestion, pointing out that by easing their labour neither so many people would earn merit, nor would those who performed the lighter task earn so much merit. A decision that compels admiration.

Mr. Parker, in his book, *Ancient Ceylon*, is convinced that Mahagama is identical with Tambapanni, where landed Wijaya,the founder of the Sinhalese race. The tradition that the name Ruhuna originated from the nephew of Wijaya tends to confirm this contention. If this theory is true, it was at Kirinda, and not near Puttalam, that Wijaya's men, wandering against his orders, one after another in pursuit of a bitch, fell into the power of a "*yakkhini*" (female devil) called Kuvanna. This incident is an early example of how breach of discipline leads to trouble; the men thought, "Only where there is a village dogs are to be found," and, as soldiers of all ages have ever done, went in search of amusement.

The *yakkhini*, who, disguised as a woman hermit, was spinning at the foot of a tree, persuaded them all to bathe in a clear pool, when, crying, "Stay! Thou art my prey!" she compelled them to stand as if bound. She could not eat them, because each wore a magic thread; instead, therefore, she cast them all seven hundred, into a chasm. Wijaya, finding that his followers were mislaid, investigated the circumstances of their disappearance and met Kuvanna. He, however, had by this time some experience in extricating his companions from embarrassing predicaments. Their voyage down the coast of India had not been uneventful; so he did not bathe when invited, but caught the *yakkhini* by her neck in the noose of his bow, held her hair and threatened her with his sword, whereat she returned his men, and fed them upon provisions looted from the ships of unsuspecting merchants whom she had devoured.

Wijaya, ever gallant, in spite of his recent violence towards her, offered the seeming elderly hermit woman the first helping—an attention so pleasing to her that she at once became a beautiful sixteen-year-old maiden. Wijaya married her without delay. Next he killed all the neighbouring *yakkhas*, in spite of their invisibility, while they were gathered at a wedding, being guided as to their whereabouts by the indications of Kuvanna, who seems to have had no scruples in betraying her relations.

After thus removing opposition Wijaya founded his city of Tambapanni (according to Mr. Parker), six miles from the mouth of the Kirinda river, then known as the Maha Kandura. The mouth of the Kirinda appears to have been the port of Ceylon for Indian traders, who went up the ancient great North road through Gutthala (Buttala), and across the Mahaveliganga at Dastota to Polonnaruwa and Anuradhapura.

Wijaya's ministers, having founded cities for themselves elsewhere in Ceylon, subsequently asked him to be their King—an invitation that he refused unless a suitable consort was provided for him. He seems to have been rather indelicately desirous of disposing of Kuvanna, who was presumably becoming a little *passé*. Messengers were sent to Pandu, King of Madura, "to woo his daughter for their Lord." The monarch thought the match a good one, so the princess, accompanied by nearly a hundred other maidens, sailed for Ceylon, with a retinue of chaperons. It is reputed that invasions of a parallel nature occur even up to the present day. Meanwhile the discarded Kuvanna was ignominiously expelled from Tambapanni by Wijaya, with the incongruous words "Go thou now, dear one." Again and again she besought him to let her remain, but she was relentlessly driven away to the *yakkha* city of Lankapura, where she met her death as a spy at the hands of a *yakkha* "who was violent."

Wijaya consecrated the Pandu princess as his Queen and reigned at Tambapanni for thirty-eight years. At his death he expressed a desire for his brother to succeed him, as he had no son of Royal blood, so Panduvasudeva was brought by messengers from India to Tambapanni, whence he journeyed for his coronation to the new capital at Upatissagama, near Anuradhapura. In the meantime, a bride was coming to join him by the same route, under romantic circumstances. Sakka Pandu, a Sakaya king, who lived "on the farther side of the Ganges," had a daughter called Bhaddakaccana. "She was even as a woman made of gold, fair of form and eagerly wooed. For love of her did seven kings send precious gifts to King Pandu." These seven rivals appeared so likely to fight among themselves, besides rendering a decision in favour of one the signal for a war with the remaining six, that Sakka Pandu was puzzled as to how to extricate himself from the difficulty. He evolved a plan which is a credit to the sporting spirit of the era. A race was instituted, combining the pleasure of yachting with the excitement of hare and hounds—the hare being Bhaddakaccana. Placing her in a boat with thirty-two women friends, the King launched it on the Ganges, saying: "Whosoever can, let him take my daughter." The hare, however, outran, or rather outsailed, the hounds at such a speed that on the second day she landed with her companions, robed as nuns, at the mouth of the Maha Kandura (or Kirinda). From there, led by feminine instinct as to where lay their rosiest prospects, they fared forth to the capital, where Bhaddakaccana married the king, and bore him ten sons and one daughter—a felicitous ending to her travels.

From this period—*i.e.*, about 440 B.C.—the more northern cities became the centre of government, and Mahagama does not figure prominently again in Ceylon history until 240 B.C., when it reappears in the following incident:

"Viharadevi was the consort of the believing King Kakavannatissa, firm in the faith was she, the daughter of the King of Kelaniya." This faithful and beautiful lady had a most romantic history. Her father, Tissa, King of Kelaniya, rejoiced in a charming Queen, who was on terms exceeding the bounds of friendship with the King's brother, Uttiya. The King realized this, so Uttiya had to leave hurriedly, taking refuge at Udugampola; however, feeling that a letter explaining his departure was due to the Queen, he employed a man disguised as a priest to carry a letter to her. This messenger entered the Royal quarters in the retinue of the Chief Priest of the Court, and managed to catch the eye of the Queen just as Tissa was leaving the room. Having attracted the lady's attention—probably by means of an unpriestly wink—he dropped the letter in her sight.

Tissa, however, who evidently watched his wife with suspicion, was not so easily outwitted. He heard the letter drop, and opened it. Its contents so infuriated him that he caused the emissary to be hewn in pieces, the Queen to be drowned in the river, and, since, the handwriting was apparently that of the real Chief Priest, he had that dignitary immersed in a cauldron of boiling oil. Afterwards the remains of all of them were thrown into the sea. In the execution of the Chief Priest the King made a mistake; it transpired that Uttiya had been taught to write by this worthy and innocent cleric, so that their styles were almost identical.

The gods were so annoyed by such off-hand treatment of the Chief Priest that they caused the sea to overflow the whole of Kelaniya. Tissa, alarmed at the floods, which are still not infrequent on the Avisawella road, cast about for a means of appeasing the gods. A solution of the problem soon occurred to him. "Quickly placing his own lovely daughter, Devi, in a golden box, whereon was inscribed 'A King's

" KING KAKAVANNATISSA OPENED THE LID "

E

daughter,'" he launched her forth upon the rising tide. She came to shore in the same place where one or two other ladies before her had landed after not dissimilar adventures, near Mahagama, in Ruhuna. A fisherman, finding the golden vessel ashore, was so honest as to report his discovery to King Kakavannatissa, who, magnanimously accepting as true the inscription upon it, opened the lid of the vessel and forthwith married its contents. The maiden's figure was lovely, and her limbs, which "were of perfect outline," epitomized the description "*adissamanasamdhi*" (with invisible joints)—conveying the idea of plumpness or good upholstering—so that possibly her dazzling beauty promoted an easy belief in her ancestry. Since she landed near a *vihare* she was called Viharadevi.

The marriage turned out a complete success, except for the fact that no son arrived to succeed the King. Viharadevi, assiduous in her almsgiving and generous care for the priesthood of Mahagama, was complimented by the chief priest upon her prosperity. She contended in reply that, in the absence of children to bless her marriage, she could not be called prosperous. The Chief Priest said: "Queen, look for the realization of your wish to the suffering *samanera*." Now at that time there had been brought to the Tissarama *vihare* at Mahagama a devout priest from Kattipabbata, where he had led a life of manifold toil, including the making of steps up to the "Akasa-cetiya" (air-sanctuary) —a shrine on the top of a rock, which still exists near Kataragama. He was now in the last stages of a serious illness from which recovery was impossible. The Queen implored him to be re-born, after his death, as her son; at first he refused to become a member of the Royal family, but at last, relaxing his determination in face of the lady's importunity, he consented, and died immediately.

It was not long before he fulfilled his promise Viharadevi very soon afterwards expressed to the King three longings:

Firstly, that, lying on her left side on a magnificent bed, with her head pillowed on a honeycomb the size of a bull, she should feed twelve thousand priests on the honeycomb, then eat the portion left by them.

Secondly, that she should bathe in the water that washed the sword that struck off the head of the chief warrior of Elara, the Tamil king then reigning at Anuradhapura. While thus bathing she wished to stand on the head of the unfortunate deceased.

Thirdly, that she might wear an unfaded garland of water-lilies, brought from the marshes of Anuradhapura.

The first of these rather capricious wishes seems to have rested for its fulfilment entirely on the chance of finding a honeycomb big enough, but the last two involved great personal risk for their executor, and a possible precipitation of the ever-threatening war with the Tamils. Such considerations, however, counted for little, especially since the fortune-tellers predicted that "The Queen's son, destroying the Damilas and reducing the country under one sovereignty, will make the religion of the land shine forth again."

A commensurate reward was offered for a honeycomb of requisite proportions, and, luckily, a man discovered a canoe on the seashore near Mahagama, overturned and filled with honey. Possibly the finder kept bees. A convenient building was erected, in which the Queen was able to gratify her first wish.

Meanwhile a warrior named Velusumana had set forth to encompass the remaining requirements. Velusumana gained the confidence of Elara's head groom by helping him in his work of looking after the Royal charger at Anuradhapura. One morning he stole the horse, without raising any suspicion, and picking up on his way a sword and a garland of lotuses, which he had previously concealed, rode off announcing his identity. At once Elara sent the leading Tamil warrior, Nandisathi, in pursuit on his second horse. Velusumana retired into a thicket, from which, as Nandisathi dashed past, he stretched forth his sword neck-high, so that the luckless Tamil's head was cut off by the force of his own impetus. Then, taking the head and garland, Velusumana returned to Mahagama the same evening—a journey of two hundred miles—thereby enabling Viharadevi to gratify all her wishes. It is satisfactory to learn that Velusumana was adequately rewarded for his noble services.

In course of time an event that seldom fails to elicit congratulation occurred in the Royal family: "200 B.C. (*circa*). At Mahagama. To Queen Viharadevi, wife of King Kakavannatissa of Ruhuna, a son."

This child, whose advent was heralded by several most unusual phenomena, including the finding of a State elephant recently born in a grove of kadol-trees, was to become the great Duttha Gamini, who defeated Elara and restored the old Sinhalese splendour of Anuradhapura. Not content with this good fortune, the Queen again presented her gratified husband with another son; this one they called Tissa—a choice more conservative than original.

Gamini and his brother differed little from other infants in showing no signs of unusual mentality until the ceremony of "giving rice," or weaning. Collecting in a golden dish a little milk rice from the half-consumed portion of five hundred priests whom he had served, the King put some of the rice into the mouth of each child, saying: "My children, if ye ever become subverters of the true faith, may this food, when admitted into your stomachs, never be digested. The two babies are said to have understood their father's meaning perfectly, but nevertheless they swallowed the rice without fear, and probably cried for more.

When the two boys became about twelve years old King Kakavannatissa tested them once more in the same way. Over the matter of religion they avidly consumed their rice, even vowing never to be enemies they gulped down a second helping—although it was not long before they were at war with one another; but when asked to eat a third helping, swearing at the same time, "We will never make war upon the Damilas," both of them refused to touch the food, not because they had already eaten too much, but because it was a matter of honour with them to extirpate the Tamils.

Gamini's conduct, in fact, forms the subject of a favourite Sinhalese story. Retiring to his bed, he lay on it curled up, in an attitude suspiciously suggestive of a severe stomach-ache, induced by his false promise at the second helping; but when asked by his anxious mother, who was evidently inclined to spoil her first-born, why he did not stretch out and lie comfortably, he stoutly replied: "When I am confined on the one side by the Damilas beyond the river, and on the other by the great green ocean, how can I lie down in so cramped a space with outstretched limbs?"

The King, on hearing this *bon mot*, was speechless with surprise.

Although Kakavannatissa was averse to a war against the Tamils, he encouraged the acquisition of a great army under Gamini's command in Mahagama. At that time one

Nandimitta lived at Anuradhapura; he was so strong when a baby that, in order to prevent him from wandering, a heavy stone was fastened to his waist by a thong ("*nandi*"). He managed to break this on the threshold of a door, and grew up as powerful as ten elephants. If a Tamil annoyed him by offering any indignity to the sacred edifices, Nandimitta used to split him in to and throw him outside the city wall, where the local "*devas*" (gods) rendered the corpse invisible. The Tamils could never find out how these men vanished, so that the frequent mysterious disappearances began to get seriously on their nerves.

Although this practice caused an "obvious diminution of the Damilas," Nandimitta felt that his success led nowhere, and saying to himself "In Ruhuna there are still princes who have faith in the three gems" (*i.e.*, the Buddha, his doctrine and his community), he left the scene of his depredations and joined Gamini's Court at Mahagama. He was the first of ten mighty warriors whom Gamini collected as the nucleus of his army. Each of these ten was capable of astounding feats of strength, speed and endurance. Velusumana was a marvellous rider; he procured for himself such remarkable mounts that when he rode one of his horses round a large ring his speed was so terrific that he looked like a continuous chain of men galloping on horses—a kind of living cinematograph film—at the same time he stood up on the horse's back untying and retying his scarf. Nimila could journey to Anuradhapura, see all the sights of that mighty city, and return to Ruhuna in a day. Sona tore up full-grown coconut-trees. Gothaka could clear a jungle in a few minutes by uprooting the vegetation. Abhaya, at twelve years old, played handball with stones that four or five normal men could not lift; when he was sixteen he had a staff thirty-eight inches in circumference and sixteen cubits long, with which he felled palmyrah- and coconut-trees at a blow. Bharana chased hares and elks and cut them in two with a single kick while on the run. Deva could whirl an ox round his head by the leg and reduce its bones to powder by dashing it to the ground. Phussadeva blew a chank, or horn made of shell, like a peal of thunder; he could also shoot an arrow with unerring aim, when guided by sound only as to the target, as quickly as lightning, and with such force that it would penetrate a cartload of sand or a plate of iron. Vasabha was as beautiful as Adonis; besides which he could lift a basket of earth "which ten or twelve stout labourers could alone raise." The word "stout" in this translation is intended to refer to the labourers' physical ability rather than to their figures.

Each of these ten chose ten other warriors, and each of that hundred ten more, until, by means of this arithmetical progression, the army numbered eleven thousand one hundred and ten men on parade when all present and correct.

Kakavannatissa sent his son, Tissa, to Dighavapi (now said to be Maha Kandiya tank in the Eastern Province) with a large army in order to protect the eastern end of Ruhuna from Tamil inroads, but Gamini lived at Mahagama in charge of the main army. He was "skilled in elephant, horse and bow exercises, as well as in stratagems," so that it was not surprising that with a well-trained army under his command he longed to fight the Tamils. King Kakavannatissa, however, persistently refused to allow a war, until Gamini, with unfilial impertinence, sent his father a woman's trinket accompanied by the message: "Since it appears that my father is not a man, let him decorate himself with a feminine ornament." The old King, very indignant, ordered a golden chain to be made in order to fetter his son, who fled in fury to the hills of Malaya or Kandy. From this discreditable incident he received the name Duttha (unfilial or inimical) Gamini.

King Kakavannatissa died, having reigned sixty-four years, while Duttha Gamini was still in exile, so Tissa performed the funeral ceremony, and returned to Dighavapi, taking with him his mother, Viharadevi, and Kandula, the State elephant.

Duttha Gamini soon heard of his father's death, and returned to Mahagama, where he established himself in his rightful position as King. His repeated demands for the return of his mother and Kandula being refused, war with Tissa was inevitable. In the ensuing battle Duttha Gamini was heavily defeated, and fled, pursued by Tissa; however, some priests, disapproving of this inter-fraternal strife, raised a mountain across Duttha Gamini's line so that Tissa lost the scent. After his return to Mahagama the defeated monarch reorganized his army, and again engaged his brother in combat. This time Duttha Gamini, on his mare, leapt right over Tissa on Kandula, passing his spear out of bravado between the elephant's armour and skin as he passed.

The elephant, enraged at being made to look a fool by a mare, tried to dislodge Tissa by rushing at a tree, but Tissa climbed up the tree and escaped. Kandula then returned to Duttha Gamini, his lawful master. It is noticeable that when these state elephants once grasped the situation they could always be relied upon to do the right thing. The unfortunate Tissa hid under the Chief Priest's bed in a neighbouring *vihare*, to which Duttha Gamini traced him by his footsteps. All the priests in the *vihara* who had been standing up sat down, and all those who had been sitting stood up, so that when questioned, all who were sitting said, "I did not see him sitting here," and all who were standing said, "I did not see him standing here."

Duttha Gamini then inquired in exasperation:

"Where *is* Tissa?" Whereto the chief priest, like Washington, unable to tell a lie, replied: "Raja, he is not *on* the bed."

Duttha Gamini, not in the least deceived, knew from the priest's ingenuous embarrassment that Tissa was *under* the bed, but, unwilling to violate the *vihara,* he left him where he was, and contented himself with placing a guard round the building. The priests endeavoured to deceive the guard by carrying out the fugutive upon their shoulders on a bed, as if he were a

[*Sketch by R.H.B.*]

"RAJA, HE IS NOT ON THE BED"

corpse, but Duttha Gamini easily penetrated this ruse, and magnanimously let his brother go, with a few taunting remarks about his unworthiness to be thus elevated above the clergy. Tissa soon repented of his insubordinate attitude towards his elder brother, and coming to Mahagama disguised as a young priest, waited until an old *thera* had paved the way for reconciliation, when, aided by the entreaties of Queen Viharadevi, he was able to make peace with Duttha Gamini.

Now that Duttha Gamini was at liberty to wage war against the Tamils without interruption, he held a great review at Mahagama. Then taking with him five hundred ascetics, who went to war as a penance, not for pleasure, he marched northwards to victory over the Damilas outside the limits of Ruhuna.

This period marks the height of interest in the history of Mahagama; it remained the capital of the Ruhuna for many hundred years, but never again sheltered personalities of such distinction as in the second century B.C. The importance of the Northern capitals first overshadowed the magnificence of Mahagama, then the withdrawal of the Sinhalese kings to the Kandyan provinces, leaving the sea-coasts at the mercy of the Portuguese and other invaders, led to the decay of its architectural magnificence and the total eclipse of its political importance.

During the Portuguese era there is little of interest to attract attention to Tissamaharama and its neighbourhood, although it is not improbable, as Pridham suggests, that the ruined condition of Mahagama is in part due to the religious fervour of the Portuguese in the destruction of Buddhist magnificence.

The Dutch, however, who were enthusiastic salt traders, knew the value of the district. A Sinhalese king, in the hope of keeping the Hollanders quiet by satisfying their desire for territory, told them that they could have the whole coast-line of Ceylon, but their claim was

KING KAKAVANNATISSA BATHING AT KIRINDA ON A COLD DAY

In order to preclude antiquarian argument as to the style of bathing dress favoured by King Kakavannatissa, he has been pictured bathing without one. The embarrassing question of Queen Viharadevi's costume does not arise, as she bathed on the other side of the rocky point.

not to exceed a distance of more than two hours' march inland. In an old Dutch map of Ceylon can be seen the Dutchmen's ostensible estimate of their own marching powers; the only charitable surmise is that they must have been prodigious walkers.

South of Tissamaharama is the village of Kirinda, which was the pleasure resort of Mahagama, although the actual seaport of the city was probably at the mouth of the Kirinda Oya. Mr. Pridham has the following description: "Kirinde is a rocky point on the coast, remarkable for the artificial appearance of its masses of stone, among which there is a spring of fresh water, also some remains of masonry; and the outline of figures of the sun and moon render probable the tradition that the kings of Magaama occasionally resorted to this spot to enjoy the cooling breeze and sea-bathing." Lieutenant Schneider states that "a post was stationed formerly here at Kieriende" to guard the salt. He refers apparently to an English military post, which probably took the place of a small Dutch guard.

On the coast, at Bundala salt-shore, there is a stone on which the Sinhalese initial "Ko" is carved. This letter began the name of a celebrated priest, who carved it when the stone formed part of the old temple. He, when a boy, had no women relations left alive, so that his father, who seems to have been a hard man, made him do all the housework, besides carrying food to the fields. The boy, growing tired of this endless labour, ran away to the jungle, where he lived with a herd of pigs, becoming in time almost one of their community. When he had grown to be seventeen or eighteen years old, a hunting party visited Bundala, and the boy, being unable to run as fast as the pigs, was captured. The unpleasant fact is reported that he was thickly covered with ticks. However, he apparently got rid of these insects in time and became a Buddhist priest, carving his initial in stone at the temple in order to commemorate his experiences. One of the elder inhabitants of Bundala can still remember him.

Hambantota, seen from the headland on which stands the lighthouse, is a very picturesque town; across the bay a vast expanse of jungle stretches unbroken to the peaks of Kataragama on the north-east and even farther, to the hills of Uva on the north. On the beach, in the curve of the bay, lie the fisherfolk's catamarans, with the market and town behind them, while once a month the *Lady McCallum* used to sail round the point to cast anchor in the harbour for a few hours, discharging her cargo. The ship, besides making a pretty picture as she steamed up to the anchorage, caused a small flutter of excitement ashore.

Lieutenant Schneider said that "this place is considered as an unwholesome one," but at the present day the town itself does not deserve that epithet. Mr. Pridham mentions Hambantota in 1815: "Between the sea and the town the enormous hills of sea-sand—upon which a heavy carriage may be driven with as much facility as on the best macadamized road—encroach so very rapidly that houses have been continually pulled down and rebuilt at a greater distance to prevent their being overwhelmed. The accumulation of sand must have been as rapid as the growth of the adjoining coconut-trees, for some of sixty feet in height are, according to Mr. Bennett, buried up to the crests, the only parts visible above the surface, and the bunches of nuts lie upon the sand as if they were the produce of a gigantic plant, instead of being the fruit of one of the tallest of the palm family, and may be cut from their stalks by a little child."

Near the lighthouse, on the promontory, stands a round Dutch tower of three storeys, built of coral stone, about fifty feet or more in diameter and approximately sixty or seventy feet high. The ground floor, which was a storehouse and dungeon, is accessible by a trap-door in the first floor, where was the loopholed guardroom, from which a flight of wooden steps inside the building leads to the flat roof with its parapet wall, where an organized defence can be maintained. The parapet wall, which overhangs the main wall, has recesses at intervals, with slots in their floors giving a clear view of the foot of the tower—thus affording facilities for shooting at, or pouring boiling liquid upon attackers who gained the base of the fortress. On the seaward side of the tower, whence attack was evidently not expected, is the entrance, still containing its solid Dutch door, gained by means of a flight of steps, so constructed as to be drawn up after the defenders were safely inside. Near the tower are the traces of foundations of old buildings, probably small barracks, while the house of the District Engineer, who uses the fortress as his office and store, is still known as "the Commandant's bungalow." The occupation by the Public Works Department ensures that the tower is kept in good repair, although it has been found difficult to keep the flat roof watertight, since the Hollanders' expensive recipe of mixing jaggery with their plaster to render it weather-proof is too extravagant to retain its popularity. The joists of the original flooring are supported in the centre of the structure by an enormous pillar about eight feet thick, round which is the rifle-rack used by the Dutch garrison of twenty or thirty men, who were kept here to guard the salt "*lewayes*" (lagoons) from depredation. From the top of the tower, in its commanding position, a perfect watch can be kept by day over the adjoining salt area.

It seems doubtful if this little fort was ever subjected to attack in Dutch times, but after it was taken over by the English it was beleagured by the Kandyans, who were beaten off by the garrison.

The Dutch conducted a bigger salt business

than is done at the present day, although there is now a large annual collection. Lieutenant Schneider did not consider that in 1807 sufficient care was taken of this industry, nor did he approve of its organization at the time. His remarks about the system have a malicious humour: "The inhabitants of this Province do not purchase salt, having sufficient opportunities to steal salt from the salt pans—as much as they want, perhaps more."

Hambantota is essentially a Malay settlement, although, due to modern traffic facilities, Sinhalese are probably numerically superior. The town remains, however, the main centre from which Malays penetrate all over Ceylon, while its local characteristics have been permeated for centuries by the sentiments of that nationality. The origin of this settlement is ascribed to the thirteenth century A.D., when Malay *prahus*, sailing to and from Madagascar—where they still have a colony—made it a practice to call at the bay for water. The few people who formed the nucleus of a small colony, finding its living in the maintenance of a port for stores at this remote spot, naturally attracted later immigrants to their neighbourhood. Sampantot (boat-place), being familiar as a port of call, then became the recognized landing place for emigrant Malays in early times.

The colony was subsequently swelled both by ex-soldiers who, on retirement from Dutch service, gravitated to their overseas home, and by the instalment there of several Malay families of good standing, who were deported by the Dutch Government from Batavia for political reasons. Probably the superannuated soldiers formed the main bulk of the colony, but authority lay with the deported Batavia families. This exiled aristocracy was led by the Dooles, whose name, combined with the ascendancy of the family in this small isolated community, recalls the infamous Doones of Blackmore's famous novel. It must, however, be emphasized that, as regards character and citizenship, the simile changes to a vivid contrast. The political outcasts were sent to Hambantota about 1740, where, owing probably to the suspicion resting upon them, they were not employed in Dutch military service. On the arrival of the English, members of the family appear in the Ceylon Regiment, both as officers and men, one of them rising to the rank of Captain. During the Kandyan war in 1803, two Malays claimed by the Dooles to be of their stock, after capture by the Kandyans, were asked to serve in the Kandyan army. They replied that, having taken the oath of allegiance to the English, they could not desert from that service. Thereupon they were given the choice of joining the Kandyan flag or having their heads cut off. They chose to be beheaded; but the Kandyan King, thinking that perhaps suffering for their cause might alter their allegiance, put them into prison for two months on very short rations.

On being taken out of prison their gallant decision remained unchanged, so they were beheaded. Without fear of being accused of overestimating their own fortitude, these two soldiers might well have gone to their death chanting the Malay charm for courage, in which occurs the "magnificent boast":

> "Of iron am I, my bones of brass,
> And my name—The Tiger of God."

At Hambantota, where their own language and customs are active, the Malays preserve their quaint national humour, as expressed in story and poem, although outside the community it is seldom encountered. Mr. R. J. Wilkinson, in his book, *Malay Subjects*, says: "Malay fables, as well as circulating all over the Malay Archipelago, and finding kindred tales in India and Tibet, have eventually a range that only conjecture can deal with, and Brer Rabbit, Reynard the Fox, and Friend Mouse-deer (the corresponding Malay animal hero) are discovered to be blood brothers, a cosmopolitan trinity." Then, in verse, of which the clever rhythm in some measure compensates for the loss of accent and gesture, he translates a Malay tale, which has its equivalent both in the adventures of the European Brer Terrapin, and also in those of an Amazon Indian tortoise.

> "Friend Mouse-deer danced upon his way
> And shunned the river many a day,
> Still fearing he despite his guile

The cruel eye of Crocodile :
Till after many weeks had fled,
The season being hot, 'tis said,
And water most inviting cool,
He ventured down beside a pool
To quench his thirst, and drinking deep
Heard not a long slow rustling creep,
That brought Friend Crocodile so near
You'd hear the trickle of his tear :
He only had to yawn and crunch
And presto Mouse-deer for his lunch.
Friend Mouse-deer turn'd ; by half-an-inch
Too late his leap, and sharp the pinch
Of cruel fangs upon his leg ;
He could not move nor stir a peg ;
Struggle and he must be a cripple,
All for the sake of that long cool tipple.
'Friend Crocodile,' he then began,
For animals could talk like man—
'Are rotten twigs such dainty ration,
That one of your exalted station
Deign to devour them ?' 'What,' growled Croc.
Feeling it now his chance to mock :
'Your leg a twig ? Ah, well I never ;
Friend Mouse-deer, you are wondrous clever.'
'Just taste,' said Mouse-deer : 'do not bite
Or you'll not get the flavour right.'
Friend Croc, straight licks, lets go his grip,
And Mouse-deer, free, with flying skip
Gains the high bank and laughing cries :
'It was my leg, you cockatrice.' " *

*With apologies to Hudibras.

There are, in this vast expanse of country, many other places notable for portentous events that have happened within their limits, but, in the words of Mr. Rudyard Kipling, "That is another story." The scene of the several incidents to which attention has been drawn is now an uninviting, and for the most part unhealthy, jungle, hiding, like the forest that screened the Sleeping Beauty, the slowly fading relics of a mighty past. "In what is now a thorny brake . . . kings and queens went, twenty centuries ago, a-pleasuring in golden chariots drawn by gaily caparisoned horses; and thickets, overgrown with weeds and underwood, haunts of the elephant, bear and leopard, occupy the sites of royal pavilions, where of old was held high festival with revelry and song."

CHAPTER FOUR

THE PORTUGUESE SOLDIER

UNTIL within the last century in Ceylon, the proverb, "An Englishman's home is his castle," could have been equally truthfully rendered, "A business man's factory is his fort." Every commercial enterprise in former times was a courageous venture, involving, in addition to financial risk, personal hazard from jealous trade rivals or outraged local susceptibilities. It does not appear that any trading post, however honestly peaceful its intentions, eventually escaped becoming a military stronghold. To some extent this unfortunate condition of affairs was due to the Portuguese, who, relying with cynical ostentation upon their motto, "Amity, commerce and religion," shamelessly converted the factories, which they established in the guise of merchants, into fortresses, where their true rôle of conquistadores soon became patent. As Sir J. Emerson-Tennent points out, their business methods were typified by the nominal excuse for these tactics, which was that they had received orders "to begin by preaching, but, that failing, to proceed to the decision of the sword." Ribeiro alludes to the trading principles of his countrymen in the nature of a joke, when referring to the concession by the Sinhalese king of all their early demands, because "it did not escape his knowledge that according to reputation we usually succeeded in obtaining whatever we sought."

The Portuguese soldier, through whose instrumentality such "demands" were possible, was an interesting type. Unlike the British troops who later met with success in the Kandyan wars, the Portuguese rank and file were the sweepings and off-scourings of the slums of Portugal—a fact which makes their amazing bravery the more remarkable. In the rank of common soldier none but the very lowest could be procured to go to death in exile, after untold hardships. In later times most of those who came on Eastern service were forced into the venture, being either kidnapped as boys or sentenced to foreign service for some crime. The life of the Portuguese soldier in Ceylon was a succession of degrading excesses in every form of vice: he was only half-clothed and ill-fed, while his officers appropriated much of his pay, yet when in one of the "tight corners" which so frequently formed his lot he acquitted himself with the utmost gallantry against overpowering odds. The Portuguese expected no quarter and gave none, only taking alive, when possible, their more eminent foes, on the principle that

A PORTUGUESE SOLDIER

they afforded better sport alive than dead. The same consideration actuated them as regards the women of their enemies, whom they did not kill at once, considering them more in the nature of loot than human beings. Discipline was harsh but efficient as far as the maintenance of an active fighting force was concerned. The fostering of an offensive spirit was well understood, and the cultivation of a code of honour as regards courage never neglected. Quarrelling and brawling in barracks received heavy punishment, but an insult had to be avenged in a formal duel, supervised by a senior non-commissioned officer, while if the aggrieved party failed to call out his enemy his career as a soldier suffered thereby. Towards the close of the Portuguese occupation, however, both discipline and personnel degenerated, especially in Colombo, where mutiny was rife and assassination the recognized channel of promotion.

Near the road from Panadura to Ratnapura, on the eastern bank of the Kalu-Ganga, at Kiriella, are the ruins of a large Portuguese fort, which, situated on high ground at a sharp bend in the stream, occupied a position combining strength with beauty. Built both to command the water highway and also as a store for areca, cinnamon and spices, it contained a fine residence for the Commandant, below whose windows, on the outer escarpment of the walls, spread a broad terrace overlooking the river and mountains of Kukul Korale. Here in the cool of the evening the Governor and his lady could withdraw from the military atmosphere within the battlements to enjoy the beauties of unrivalled tropical scenery. Along the river frontage, of some sixty paces, the walls were constructed at the top of the bank, which was strengthened and protected from erosion by a curtain of huge rocks, brought from a distance by elephants, and pushed into the edge of the river until the top of the pile rose above the surface of the water. The stronghold was rectangular, with bastions at all except the south-east corner, whence the road from the gate in the eastern wall led down to the bank of the river, where, close under the wall of the fort, the ferry-boat was drawn in for protection.

To the north-west the parade-ground was artificially levelled, while to the west and east of the fort were two deep *elas*, formerly joined by a ditch. Since it was the duty of the Commandant of Kiriella to supervise the collection of jaggery and areca, which were obtained in great quantities from Kukul Korale, the fort was of considerable importance, and would, therefore, have contained a garrison kept as far as possible up to full strength : such a complement of men is said by Ribeiro to have amounted to "700 people, which was the usual full number. They were paid on two days in the year at . . . Christmas and at the Feast of San João, and the money was meant to supply the soldiers with clothing. For his sustenance, His Majesty allowed each, whatever his position, one *pardao* the month for extras and one and a half measures of rice a day, both of these being given into the hands of the captains, who gave the soldiers cooked food three times a day . . . Each of them [the captains] had two villages allotted to him for the purpose and . . . the mayorals used to provide the companies with cows, hens, chickens, butter, spices and all other necessaries, the money being supplied them for these articles by the captains."

"The soldiers were not obliged to remain in the company more than six months—that is, from one pay-day to another—when . . . they were free to join any company they selected, and as the captains used to supply the soldiers with their food, and as several of them did not do so in a reasonable fashion, and as, at the same time, it was considered a disgrace to complain about the food supplied by one's captain, all of them found their remedy in this opportunity which was allowed them. None the less every captain had the same number of soldiers as the rest; for the Captain-General used to revise the lists of the companies and take the total of all and divide them equally among the companies at the rate of thirty-six or thirty-eight each, making them all equal more or less; but the captain who had the better reputation obtained the better following and the other received the worse."

Probably owing to the fact that the Captain

of Kiriella had the handling of valuable merchandise he was a very wealthy man, and so acquired an exceptionally stalwart garrison. His house was furnished with gold beds and plate, carven tables, chairs of costly timber, and magnificent ornaments looted from the temples he had sacked. When the Dutch approached Colombo the Captain of Kiriella had to retire to aid in the defence of the capital, leaving the fort to the mercy of his enemies. Before going he caused all his priceless belongings, including a golden "*punawa*" (vessel surrounded with twelve hooded-cobra heads), to be cast into the pool below the fort, where the water was so deep that three reels of thread could not reach the bottom. Colour is lent to this story by the fact that a brass Portuguese cannon was found wedged in the rocks at the water's edge when the river was exceptionally low. The treasures have never been recovered, but at night, in the dark of the moon, the heads of the twelve cobras may sometimes be seen glimmering above the surface of the river, while the hollow sound caused by the curved palms of bathers beaten upon the water echoes from the rocks below the fort, where the ghosts of long-dead Portuguese soldiers play among the deep shadows. Occasionally, too, in the darkness the highest palm-trees are shaken by these warriors of old, who, rather than wait for nuts to be plucked, shake the trees with their giant strength until the ripe fruit falls to the ground.

Frequent expeditions into Kukul Korale were necessary to enforce the collection of produce; on these marches the soldier carried his rice in a "*bat-mallè*" (bag), made by doubling the sheathlike part of an areca leaf and tying the two ends together, as it is done at the present day. One gigantic member of the garrison, having eaten his meal, threw away the *mallè*, where it still lies, turned to a massive rock in the depths of the Korale; the place where the corner of the *bat-mallè* was cut off to extract the rice can still be seen, as well as the marks where the neck was tied. Later, getting tired of his walking-stick, which was as thick as a palm-tree, this giant soldier threw that away too; it also was turned to stone, and is now used as an "*edanda*" (bridge across a stream).

In the following story, which is based on historical fact, an attempt is made to portray the life of a Portuguese soldier in the East:

"SOUSINHA"

Manoel de Sousa, at the age of eighteen, undersized, sallow and furtive, was a miserable example of slum humanity in the seventeenth century. Since escaping from the draggled skirts of his mother he had pursued the career of a sneak-thief as his means of livelihood, until, as he sat on the doorstep of a house of very ill-fame in the lowest quarter of Oporto, a suave, swarthy ruffian of military aspect approached him. "Senhor"—the compliment did not even stir a smile—"I can show you better lodgings than these. Do you want a life of loot, women, wine, high pay, and no limit to your pleasure? What of the Golden East? The spices, dusky women and treasures of kings? I can guide you there. Will you take my offer, or will you go on rotting in this sewer, to die in jail?"

Manoel had seen others take the bait, and several times had only narrowly escaped the depredations of military kidnapping parties, but his empty stomach, and the recent activities of certain of his enemies, combined to make him follow this apostle of the Orient. His action was not blind: he knew the horrors of the voyage that awaited him, and the peril of Eastern military service, but, already inured to the worst imaginable conditions, he accepted the risk for the prospect of occasional prosperity. The stinking, insect-infested hold of a vessel in the harbour seemed, by comparison with his late surroundings, almost luxurious, while idleness and a daily filled stomach suited his ambitions to perfection. But at length the day of departure arrived, bringing with it the last passengers, most of them, except a few recruits like himself, unconscious either from drink or as a result of the attentions of the press-gang. A large proportion of the new arrivals were convicted criminals, upon whom had been passed the most terrible sentence known to Portuguese law, that of banishment to the Eastern Colonies.

With them came three women, brazen and foul-mouthed, but stalwart hussies, who fell even more readily than some of the men into the category of "hard cases." One of these women, not more than twenty-five years old, dirty and utterly without morals, attracted Manoel sufficiently to inspire in him a rough friendship, which eventually developed into a fonder emotion.

As usual, after the ship had been at sea a month or more, deaths began to occur; scurvy, and various kinds of foul diseases, contracted before the commencement of the voyage, thrived in the conditions of filth prevailing on the vessel, taking their toll of the passengers. Soon Catherina, Manoel's companion, was the only woman left, but eventually she fell ill of a violent fever, lying for days on the verge of death, helpless on a coil of rope. Manoel, showing signs of decency, inherited, perhaps, from his unknown father, tended her with what care he could, instead of throwing her aside to die, as his companions, who had no use for a sick woman, would have done. Aided by her habitual familiarity with hardship he managed to save her life, defending her during convalescence against the attentions of his fellows, at the risk of his own safety.

On rounding the Cape those capable of reaching the deck performed the time-honoured ceremony of throwing their spoons into the sea, in order to signify their arrival in the East, where the Portuguese ate his daily ration with his fingers. Emancipated from the gutter, Manoel entered the Eastern Empire as Senhor Manoel da Sousa da Villa Vicosa, a title which he upheld effectively by violence amid his friends of equally recent aristocratic origin. Owing to the ravages of disease and the homicidal character of its freight, a ship very seldom carried to Goa more than half the complement with which it started the voyage, while most of those who survived the journey were in a miserable state of health on arrival.

Manoel, whose hardened constitution stood the trip without difficulty, found himself immediately shipped to Colombo, where men were always needed for the prosecution of the everlasting war in Ceylon. He thus was not separated from Catherina, who was bound for the same destination, in the hope, which was not likely to be disappointed, of finding someone who would support her, in spite of her very positive past.

Finding on arrival as a "*reynol*" (rookie) that his services as a soldier were not immediately required, Manoel supplemented the insufficient means that he earned as a "*chetty*" (hawker) by begging and stealing as opportunity offered. To this occupation he was driven, since the Portuguese Government, whose object was to maintain only an adequate number of colonists in Ceylon for emergencies, neither guaranteed continuous military service, nor took steps to support those of its compulsory emigrants who were not in immediate employment. As a result, there was always a liberal sprinkling of the scum of Portugal loafing round Colombo, in an atmosphere of unutterable vice and squalor. Manoel, an expert in the art of leading such an existence, found life easier than at home. Catherina, the only new Portuguese woman to come to the colony for more than a year, became the object of active rivalry, but eventually fell into the possession of a rich and debauched captain, whose proprietorship was surreptitiously treated by Manoel with complete disregard.

At last, in answer to a proclamation announcing that a draft was needed for the Sabaragamuwa army, Manoel presented himself at military headquarters, where he was armed with an arquebus and pike, while for his bodily defence a leathern jerkin was issued to him, as a protection against sword-cuts and arrows. Then, commanded by an officer, the party of recruits negotiated the arduous march to Sabaragamuwa Fort, which stood near the modern Ratnapura. Here, in constant skirmishes with the Kandyan king's outposts, Manoel rose to the heights of heroism, and sank to the brutal excesses of which the Portuguese in the East were capable. Always fearless and unruly among his companions, in war he displayed such unbridled ferocity that the nickname of "*Sousinha*" ("Little Lion"), by which he was known on account of his small size became a word of terror among the outlying Kandyan posts. He earned promotion and the title of "Cavalheiro Fidalgo" for distinguished valour; while in the course of numerous raids he acquired enough loot to ensure at least a few months of luxury when the time came to demand discharge. After two years the military distinction which he had won made it possible for him to manoeuvre his return to Colombo, where he immediately set to work to realize his fortune. Having engaged a crier, whom he decked with all his looted jewellery, he followed him forth to parade the main street at the "*leilao*" (daily auction), where the stolen valuables fetched a price that enabled Manoel to fulfil the long-desired ambition of appearing in public habited as befitted so eminent a warrior. After completing the purchase of an outfit of ultra-fashionable clothing, and with five hired men attending upon him, he walked abroad in a stately panoply that brought bliss to his ill-balanced soul.

It was thus that Catherina, resting one evening in her cloth and jacket behind the *tat* which covered her window, beheld a gorgeous apparition approaching the house. The diminutive stature of the central figure was more than counterbalanced by the magnificence of his apparel. A huge sombrero hat obscured his face in dense shadow, from which extended a handsome tobacco pipe, with a gracefully curved stem of such exaggerated length as had rarely been seen, even in the most advanced circles of Portuguese fashion. A voluminous scarlet cloak was saved from trailing in the mud by the offices of an attendant, while the brilliantly slashed doublet surmounted a dazzling pair of hose, which disappeared into deerskin boots with elegantly flapped tops. An obsequious dependent bore the exquisite's sword, another his umbrella, a third his tinder and tobacco, while a fourth paraded solemnly behind, ready to render assistance to his master in any capacity that might be required. The procession advanced with pompous slowness, each step taken by its principal occupying some seconds of ostentatious deliberation. The salutation of a friend was a matter of majestic decorum, in which the faintest suggestion of haste was a personal affront, only to be avenged by the steel of a hired assassin.

When at length the party arrived Catherina was not surprised to see the Senhor glance boldly at her window—it was a habit many young men of the city had acquired—but her cry of delighted amazement was genuine when she recognized in this splendid cavalier the dirty little vagabond who was the only man for whom she had ever felt any affection. Manoel had not expected any sign from the window, but on returning to his quarters he found, as he hoped, a female slave bearing a message which assigned a meeting-place for that very night. After this reunion the interrupted course of their relationship was resumed, regardless of Catherina's husband, who solaced his injured vanity elsewhere.

At Manoel's rate of living a reimbursement of his finances soon became necessary; for this purpose the acquisition from the Government of a rich village, by a soldier of his reputation, was not a difficult matter. On the proceeds of produce, mercilessly extorted from the inhabitants, he could have lived for some time in affluent ease, but he was never able to enjoy the fruits of his estate, owing to the advent of the Hollanders, whose activities now began to occupy the entire attention of the Portuguese. The power of Portugal had been for some time on the wane, due largely to the corrupt inefficiency of the Government, from the Viceroy downwards. Forts were in disrepair, and in many cases ungarrisoned, while rancour amounting to mutiny existed in the badly equipped and erratically paid army. But, with the enemy almost at their gates, the Portuguese rallied as usual, and exerted their utmost powers to repair the neglected fortifications of Colombo. Women and children, even of the highest ranks, joined in the labours where they could, serving not only as auxiliaries, but actually toiling at the manual labour of earth and stone-work. In these frenzied preparations Manoel took a prominent part, his natural military ability, combined with the experience gained in his two years' campaigning, qualifying him for a responsible position in the garrison. Accordingly, promoted to the rank of Captain, he organized the repair of San João Bastion, where the principal enemy pressure was expected, while Catherina, with romantic devotion, fashioned sticks for revetting purposes, upon the same earthwork. The Hollanders, who had held Galle and Negombo for some time, now captured Kalutara and were advancing upon Colombo, when Captain-Major Gaspar Figuira sallied forth to meet them with nine hundred of the best Portuguese troops.

After inflicting a heavy defeat on this force, the Dutch invested the city, anticipating that it would not hold out for any length of time, but the Portuguese, rising to the occasion with the courage which characterized them at that time, in spite of their decadent habits, put up one of the most gallant defences in military history. Four months of siege during the year 1635 produced an acute shortage of provisions, whereupon the Captain-General ordered the expulsion from the city of eight thousand non-combatants, who had been admitted at the first alarm. This relieved the drain upon the food supplies, but the unfortunate people who were driven out were not allowed by the Dutch to pass their lines, nor by the Portuguese to re-enter the city, so that all died of starvation or committed suicide below the walls. It was not surprising, therefore, that, with these vast numbers of unburied dead in close proximity, a plague followed, which carried off the defenders in hundreds. Starvation eventually reached such a pitch that cannibalism was rampant, while the complete absence of rain rendered the heat intolerable and the stench of the corpses overpowering. Manoel and his gallant Commander were among the few officers left, while, of the women, the hardened Catherina was almost alone capable of activity. A demand for surrender was refused, with the courteous reply that until compelled to yield by lack of means of defence the Captain-General was responsible for the fort to the King of Portugal.

But meantime, in addition to attacks from every side, the exhausted garrison were threatened by a mine below the San Joâo Bastion. Manoel, who had led numerous sorties—in the course of which the Hollanders had learnt, like the Sinhalese, to dread the name of "Sousinha" —undertook to excavate a counter-gallery in order to check this manoeuvre. One afternoon, when a meeting between the two tunnels was imminent, he worked through the final intervening space himself, and broke in upon the Dutchmen with rapid pistol-fire, from the small round hole which he had made. In the pitch-darkness of the narrow Portuguese gallery men could not be seen, but in the larger Dutch tunnel they made so easy a mark that at length the Hollanders built a bullet-proof barricade of loopholed timber across the passage. Manoel immediately had a barrel of power buried on the Portuguese side of the block, with the end of the match projecting, then broke down the sides of his gallery until there was only just room for one man to wriggle on his stomach down the long dark hole. Leaving two men on guard, the survivors of the party crept out of the burrow, their clothes scraped off them, bleeding profusely from elbows and knees and with their eyes bloodshot and blinded by the fumes of powder. However unpleasant or dangerous the duty, the necessity of guarding the tunnel was obvious, in order to prevent it from becoming an aid rather than a hindrance to the Hollanders; but the selection of men to perform the task was a matter of such difficulty that the Captain-General himself picked out a reliable guard from the volunteers who offered themselves. Under the direction of Manoel a place was excavated near the Dutch block, where a man could turn round, and here the first sentry lay, peeping from behind a low barricade of earth at the Dutch barrier, while in the rear of him the second sentinel was concealed among some boards. It was the duty of the first guard, if the Dutch broke through, to fire the cask of powder, thereby blowing into eternity himself, his companion and the Hollanders.

For three months Manoel took his regular relief at the block, but as time went on fewer and fewer men remained to face the horror of the tunnel. Some were shot at the sentry post, but more deserted, until at last, after five rosters had been exhausted, Manoel and two others—Francisco Pereira, and a Sinhalese captain named Hendrick—were left to keep up the guard. It thus became impossible for these three to do anything but solitary sentry work, with an occasional snatch of sleep on the surface where constant bombardment was in progress.

At the beginning of May, Manoel lay sleeping out his period off duty on a mat, in the furnace-heat of a mudhut which served as a guardroom. His face, below the coat of grime which covered it, was parchment-white from lack of air and sun, his emaciated body covered with raw sores, and his temper blasphemously irritable. Beside him, a huddle of bones and rags, sat the once handsome Catherina, waiting with some pieces of dog's flesh to alleviate the hunger of the sleeper when he awoke. As the time for him to relieve Pereira drew near Manoel turned, seized the unappetizing food and gulped it down, while Catherina told him of the misfortunes that attended the Portuguese arms on the surface.

"Did you say that the Captain-General spoke of surrender ?" snapped Manoel. "What, then, is the use of all our sufferings ? He might have surrendered at the outset. I will not submit, to be triumphed over by these Dutch louts. If you intend to become a plaything of the Hollanders, go with the weaklings who cannot stand a little hardship until our relief comes from Goa : if you would rather die come and die with me."

Rising, Manoel left the hut with a curt nod to the woman, and, flinging himself face downwards, began his long crawl along the gallery. As the darkness closed upon him the heat became all but intolerable; with sense of direction gone, breathing in broken gasps, while the sweat streamed from his body, he elbowed his way through the burrow in an agony of effort. After some distance he wormed past an obstacle which had done more than anything else to cause desertion among the carefully selected guards. This was a soul-sickening contraction of the passage where, with desperate exertion, it was just possible for a man to squeeze through a rocky aperture which threatened to collapse at any moment, crushing and burying the person who brought about its downfall. With a profane jest upon his panting lips Manoel at last wriggled up to the recess where Pereira lay behind the barricade of earth. The retiring sentry's departure was a nightmare business, in the course of which part of the body was, for a brief period, exposed to the fire of the Hollanders. Several sentries had met their death in this manoeuvre, but Manoel and his two remaining companions had become expert in avoiding the inevitable bullet, and so far none of them had been hit.

"It seems as if these Hollanders like the place as little as we do," whispered Pereira; "there are new men every time I come. The guard on duty now took over only about an hour ago."

Preparatory to his departure Pereira threw a clod of earth into the tunnel ; as he expected, the answer was a flash from each of the two loopholes in the barrier, as both Dutch sentries emptied their muskets harmlessly, hoping to find the retiring Portuguese. But at the same moment a shot rang out from Manoel's pistol, eliciting a dull thud as one of the Hollanders fell, his forehead penetrated by a bullet fired through the loophole before he could stoop into shelter.

Meanwhile Pereira was getting away at the utmost speed, but he had not reached safety when one of the enemy, of quicker wits than the rest, fired another shot into the tunnel. A yell of agony, followed by a stream of oaths, proclaimed that the bullet had found its mark.

"Where are you hit ?" called Manoel. Amid a profusion of invective the unfortunate Pereira explained what portion of his anatomy had suffered. "As there is no sitting accommodation in this accursed hole your wound will not inconvenience you much," replied Manoel.

After this episode no sound disturbed the profound stillness of the gravelike burrow for several hours, except an occasional shot from Manoel, who well knew the value of an untiring offensive. But late in the evening loud cheers resounded from the Dutch gallery, with jeering cries of: "Come out, Rat. You have surrendered." Indications of the guard's retirement became audible, which Manoel interpreted as a ruse to make him put his head up, but when no further move was made, after the noise of the retiring guard had died away, he began to fear that their raillery had been based upon truth.

He was debating as to how to discover the real state of affairs without leaving his post, when he heard the sound of someone wriggling down the passage behind him. Ever on the lookout for treachery, he called to the newcomer, and waited, pistol in hand.

Catherina's voice answered him in weak gasps: "Manoel, is that you? I can't come much farther. They have surrendered, but I would not go out with them. I came to tell you, as you said I should."

Reaching out an arm, Manoel pulled Catherina's limp sweating body in beside him.

"Is it true then? Did not Francisco Pereira speak against it?"

"Yes, he suggested that the women should be shut in the church and burnt, while the men died fighting in a sortie on the Dutch camp. But the Bishop forbade that, so to-morrow the garrison give themselves up soon after dawn."

"Pereira was right," said Manoel; "but you, Catherina, will you die with me in this death-trap that I have defended for so long?"

Catherina's passionate reply was sufficient. A few minutes later a blinding flash, followed by a dull rumbling explosion, as Manoel fired his pistol into the powder cask, made a fitting funeral salute for two of Colombo's corrupt but heroic defenders.

CHAPTER FIVE

FORTALEZA

IT is unavoidable that the subject of fortresses in Ceylon should be approached from a Portuguese point of view, especially since it was that nation who introduced the art of scientific military engineering into the Island, and who selected most of the positions which have been subsequently held by other races. The Sinhalese of old had strongholds, but these relied mainly either upon the natural inacessibility of their positions or the vast numbers of their garrisons. They were places of retirement in time of danger rather than defensive works constructed to enable a small garrison to command a desirable trade centre against numerically superior forces. The Portuguese, with a few hundred men, held at bay armies as large as those of Duttha Gamini, thanks to their knowledge of the art of fortification, in fact at one time they held a line of forts up to the Uva boundary. The distance apart at which these redoubts were built was, according to the military policy of de Sa, a famous Portuguese Governor, not more than one day's march; but in spite of this precaution, although on several occasions armies penetrated into Uva, service in the Saparagamuwa army was constantly attended with even greater danger than elsewhere.

The Dutch too at one time occupied several fortresses in the "Saparagamuwa" area. In 1664 Raja Sinha asked his "beloved Hollanders" to assist him in crushing his rebellious subjects, but the Dutch at the time had troubles of their own to occupy them. This, however, did not deter them from offering their help a year later, when there was no longer any need for it. With great emphasis upon the loyal support they were rendering, in 1665 the Dutch occupied the territory of Raja Sinha, as far as the Uva limits, but, owing to illfeeling in Government circles, this extension of occupied territory was reported in an unfavourable light to the home Government, not as an act of aggression, but as exceeding the instructions for the development of the colony. The latter view of the affair was supported, and in 1690 all the garrisons were withdrawn to the coastal territory.

A traveller going up-country through Ratnapura will find himself following very nearly the route of the Portuguese armies. The *Ceylon Calender for the Year of Our Lord* 1819, in its "Remarks upon the Country from Colombo to Kandy," describes the beginning of the journey in terms equally applicable in 1929. "From

Colombo to Pannebakery, distance: 4 miles, the road good, with houses and coconut plantations the whole way. From Pannebakery to Kadoowella, 6 miles, the road good in dry weather, but after rains the country is subject to be overflowed by the rising of the Kelana Gonga."

The first fortress on the road is at Kaduwela, but on the opposite bank of the Kelani river, only five miles from Colombo, lies the village of Kelaniya, whose importance claims an early digression from the military path.

In very far-off times the kingdom of Kelaniya was of great size, and the city was sixteen miles from the mouth of the river, but owing to an unfortunate mistake of King Kelani Tissa, who reigned about 300 B.C., the sea is now within four miles. The immediate cause of the catastrophe was, as previously related, that the King inadvertently boiled a perfectly innocent priest in oil. Even if the victim had been guilty, it was not a compliment to the cloth, but owing to his innocence the gods were so annoyed that they caused the sea to submerge one thousand four hundred and forty-nine villages. In addition to this calamity King Kelani Tissa himself was drowned when he went to try to check the water, because the public, rightly exasperated, said that the authorities ought to do something.

If the writings of a priest, who described the place six hundred years ago, are not to be accused of exaggeration, the city was built in exact duplicate, half on each side of the river. The northern half was known as Raja Maha Kelaniya, and the southern half as Kit Siri Mevan Kelaniya, after its builder, who reigned in A.D. 301.

The river is sanctified by the Buddha's choice of this place at which to bathe, during one of his visists to Ceylon.

A peacock, who flew on a tour over the low country, from Gampola, has written in glowing terms of the endless streets of gorgeous palaces, the numerous temples and vast storehouses of mighty Kelaniya, amid which moved monarchs in Royal pomp, wealthy merchants, and the pious priesthood. The bird, being quite human, although of poetic vision, also describes in thrilling detail the social attractions of the city, which was celebrated for its high standard of feminine beauty, excelling even that of Bulatgama, "where sport the golden-bangled girls" whose "eyes amorous with lotus vie." Life in ancient Kelaniya offered much that can be appreciated.

It is interesting to observe the essential points of perfect beauty according to Sinhalese standards, as related by Dr. Davy, who appears to have taken an even more lively interest in the matter than he did in all else that he saw around him. He says: "The Sinhalese women are generally well made, and well looking, and often handsome. Their countrymen, who are great connoisseurs of the charms of the sex, and

"THE SHOT STRUCK THE KING ON THE HEAD"

H

who have books on the subject, and rules to aid the judgment, would not allow a woman to be a perfect belle unless of the following character, the particulars of which I shall give in detail, as they were enumerated to me by a Kandyan courtier, well versed and deeply read in such matters:

"'Her hair should be voluminous, like the tail of a peacock; long, reaching to the knees, and terminating in graceful curls; her eyebrows should resemble the rainbow; her eyes, the blue sapphire and the petals of the blue manilla-flower. Her nose should be like the bill of the hawk; her lips should be bright and red, like coral on the young leaf of the iron-tree. Her teeth should be small, regular, and closely set, and like jessamine buds. Her neck should be large and round, resembling the berrigodea. Her chest should be capacious; her breasts, firm and conical, like the yellow cocoanut, and her waist small—almost small enough to be clasped by the hand. Her hips should be wide; her limbs tapering; the soles of her feet without any hollow, and the surface of her body in general, soft, delicate, smooth, and rounded, without the asperities of projecting bones and sinews.'"

In 1551 a most unfortunate accident occurred at Kelaniya; as is usual in the case of a serious mishap, there are several versions of the same affair, but, whoever was to blame, the regrettable fact remains that King Bhuvaneka Bahu, "while on a water-party" with some Portuguese, was killed, "by a gentleman of that race," as Casie Chitty genteelly expresses it. The old man went to Kelaniya, convalescent after fever, and, according to the *Rajawaliya*, "he opened the doors of the uppermost storey of the Royal pavilion built over the water; and as he walked about, looking up and down the river, the Portuguese fired a shot which struck the King on the head and instantly killed him. Some say that this hurt was done of set purpose; others that it was done unwittingly: God alone knoweth which is true." Queyroz, a Portuguese historian, says that one Antonio de Barcelos was the offender, and that he confessed, when dying, that he shot at a pigeon and hit the King.

Churches were built by the Portuguese on the sites of the old temples. The positions of these places of worship are still pointed out, and the northern river bank, at a small cape which juts out into the stream, is littered with carved stones, traces of former magnificence. Under water in the river there is said to be a Buddha's footprint exactly like the one on the top of Adam's Peak, but the river has to be very low before it can be seen. The sanctity of the place is such that the early Christian missionaries complained that its influence was a distinct check upon the success of their efforts. The present temple, with its adjoining *dagoba*, contains a sixteenth-century inscription, as well as a stone *sannas*, in which the sculptor has unwisely introduced mention of a grant of land by the British Government, thus shattering its claim to antiquity.

At Kaduwela is the site of a fort, built by King Raja Sinha I. in 1559, to defend the road to Sitawaka, after he had won a great battle over the Portuguese near Mulleriyawa. Here, " King Raja Sinha, mounted on his horse, galloped throughout thc host and urged on the fight. The battle was like a show of fireworks, and smoke from the discharges of the muskets resembled mists in early Durutu. Blood flowed like water on the field of Mulleriyawa. There fell of the Portuguese army 1,600." Kaduwela had been held before as an outpost, but this was the first time that a regular fort was constructed there. The Kottugodella (Fort Hill) overlooks the road from a considerable height, continuing back for about half-a-mile to the south. As the hill is steep, it was difficult to attack on all sides, except along the hilltop, so to strengthen this flank the Portuguese, while in possession, dug a deep moat through the hill, cutting off the position from its dangerous line of approach. In 1632 the Sinhalese finally lost Kaduwela, after which it was held with a small garrison at intervals up till British times, when the Reverend Cordiner mentions a party of twenty-five sepoys and fifty armed lascorins " stationed at Kadavilly " in 1803.

On the edge of the Kelani, near the ninth mile-post, is Kanwidgala—the rock bored like an ear for jewellery. From here a massive chain was taken diagonally downstream, supported half-way across by a stone pillar, now vanished, to Galahitiyawewatta, on the opposite bank, where it was attached to another massive stone holdfast, which still stands there. When the river is low the hole in Kanwidgala is above the water, while the owner of Galahitiyawewatta says that, when he was a boy, he used to find bits of the old chain at the water's edge. There is a tunnel a little farther up-stream, whence King Raja Sinha fired a shot from a concealed cannon, which hit a floating castle contrived by the Portuguese, and wrecked their scheme of attacking Rakgahawatta. This last fortress was built by Raja Sinha I. to command the passage of the Kelani. Although all traces of the building are demolished, its site, at the junction of the Rakgahawatta *ela* with the river, is still called Pelawila Kottuwa—a name derived from a rock farther north, to which it was connected by an earthen ramp, now regarded as a "*we kanda*" (tank bund). To the west of Pelawila Gala lies Ganegala, a mass of rock used by both Raja Sinha I. and Raja Sinha II. as a base during their operations against Colombo. Upon its summit was a palace, of which the pillar sockets are in evidence. In order to overcome the discomfort of rough and uneven stone floors the chambers of the building were paved with clay, in which were embedded stones of varying sizes. This substance still adheres to the rock in several places; it must have had a smooth coating of mud, since at present its surface is far rougher than that of the bare rock. There is said to have been a fish or crocodile carved near the palace, but this has disappeared. A metal quarry has made vast inroads into Ganegala, but fortunately work has stopped before the foundations of Raja Sinha's palace were removed to be ground beneath the tyre of the motor-'bus. The people of the neighbouring village are "*achari*" (smith-folk), who were brought here to make weapons for Raja Sinha's

FACSIMILE OF THE SIGNATURE OF RAJA SINHA II.

armies. In 1656 the Dutch General Hulft came to report to the Sinhalese King his successful prosecution of the siege of Colombo. The meeting was either at Ganegala or Pelawila Kottuwa, where the palace answers more to the description of Raja Sinha's residence at the time. Hulft, soldier, sailor and trader, as occasion demanded, with his pride in his pocket and his tongue in his cheek, displayed the utmost humility—an art at which the Hollanders excelled when it suited their purposes. He knelt before the King expounding an effusive valediction, in which, among many other equally flattering phrases, he mentioned that His Majesty's name was known throughout the world. Vanity was Raja Sinha's weak spot; flattery would sometimes succeed with him where reason could not do so. His signature alone exhibits the love of display which characterized his composition.

Two miles south of Kaduwela is a place called Malwatta ("The Flower Garden"). Here, upon a large rock, is an inscription of four lines, illegible for the most part, but readable in its last lines as "*wahapia*" (hidden). Two yards to the west of the lettering is the imprint of a bull's foot, two yards to the north a hole, cut about a foot square, and six yards to the north-east a well-carved conventional lotus. Near at hand, though covered with earth or jungle, is reputed to be the impression of a human foot. These symbols are said to be the clues as to the whereabouts of a hidden treasure. Some time ago, in a record of hiding-places, an enterprising person thought he located Malwatta, but, although he took an impression of the inscription in wax, he had to admit defeat, with the ingenious but gallant excuse that since it was a princess's treasure it was safe from discovery.

From Kaduwela it is not a long journey to Bomiriya, where a side-lane leads to Raxapana ("Work-Water") ferry. This name has an interesting legendary derivation. At one time the Kelani was so low that it dried up, except for a deep pool below the great rock that juts out into the stream at this place. Everyone, therefore, on his way to or from work, had to come here to drink, so it was called "Work-Water"; probably the explanation is an etymological inaccuracy, but nevertheless attractive. Across the ferry, in Malwana, at the bend of the river, is the fort of S. Elena, originally Sinhalese, but captured and rebuilt by the Portuguese in 1593. The trace of the redoubt still exists, about sixty yards square, with angular bastions at the corners; the Kelani on the western flank, a deep *ela* on the north, and a smaller channel on the south, while the east is, as Ribeiro says, "undefended." The *cabook* walls stand to a height of two or three feet in several places.

During the government of the infamous Don Jeronimo de Azavedo, Malwana grew to be of paramount importance. Considering it more central than Colombo, he maintained his head-quarters here for nine years, establishing a Judicial Court and vast elephant stables, probably on the flat ground near the fort. In 1603, while his house was left in charge of a few servants, there was a sudden rebellion in Malwana district. Although some soldiers hurried to the rescue, they all fell in its defence, and the rebels, setting fire to the thatch covering a hole in the roof, gutted the building. While resident at Malwana, de Azavedo practised most appalling cruelties. Among others, whose atrocity renders description unnecessary, was that of throwing people from Raxapana rock into the river, where the crocodiles had become so accustomed to their regular meals that they came when they heard a whistle.

Barring the Kelani at Mapitigama a boom was fixed, during the wars of 1595, connected by canes to a bell on Raxapana, so that if a boat tried to come downstream in the dark it was both held up and gave the alarm at the same time.

Mr. E. Reimers, Government archivist, brought from The Hague a copy of an account of the fort at Malwana, dated 1624, and written in the handwriting of de Sa. In his description, de Sa mentions that the house where de Azavedo lived was occasionally submerged by floods, so, he says: "I have built my residence at Sasapana, on the side of the river, at a spot where the high water does not come." The *cabook* walls of this building—locally known as the Maligawa—still stand on an elevation behind Raxapana rock, where they are shown with great pride by the owner of the land, who has removed a number of blocks, including carved pillar capitals, to build a new house. The walls of the Government House, of great thickness, were covered with plaster, ornamented with a dado of broken oyster-shells, pressed into the wet surface, rather after the pattern of the mirror bathrooms of Akbar's queens in Agra. In these sumptuous lavatories, when his already numerous harem bathed, they were multiplied by thousands on the walls, in countless fragments of looking-glass, inlaid like mosaic. The Emperor, who was presumably the only spectator admitted, must have felt hopelessly outnumbered. It appears as if de Sa's residence suffered the same fate as that of dè Azavedo, since the roof is gone and the interior is filled with earth and rubbish. But a little excavation reveals charred rafters, lying as they fell, amongst blackened, broken earthenware, and pieces of calcined bones, possibly those of the incinerated inhabitants.

Hanwella's history as a fort continues until 1819, or later, so that its fame is not yet altogether forgotten. The comfortable resthouse on the river bank is known to most travellers, with its pleasant view, stone garden-seats, and trees planted by King Edward VII. when Prince of Wales, but the same piece of ground has been in the past the scene of many a grim struggle. Until comparatively recent times Hanwella was called Gurubewila, and under this name it figures in 1539, when the first of a long series of battles between the Sinhalese and Portuguese was fought there. With the turn of their fortunes, in 1595, the Portuguese endured a long siege in Gurubewila, when famine forced a remnant of three hundred and fifty-four men, escorting the Sinhalese King and Queen, to evacuate the fortress in an attempt to march to Colombo *via* Horana, through country

CAPTAIN POLLOCK

occupied by the enemy. Their gallant attempt was on the verge of failure as reinforcements arrived, after all but fifty men had been killed or wounded.

The Dutch, while holding this fort, suffered even worse than the Portuguese. At that time there was no well inside the walls and man after man was lost in the courageous attempt to bring in water from outside. At last thirst drove the garrison to make terms. The Sinhalese agreed to send all the wounded in barges down the Kelani to Colombo, while the active troops would be taken alive to imprisonment in Kandy. In view of these promises, the Dutch capitulated, but, after being allowed to leave the walls, all, both wounded and unwounded, were massacred, to the number of about one hundred.

After the arrival of the English, Cordiner relates that "on the morning of the 21st August (1803) a large body of the enemy (Kandyan army) had advanced within fifteen miles of the seat of Government. The night before they took the little fort of Hangwell." It was recovered on the 22nd by Lieutenant C. W. Mercer, of the 51st Regiment, who continued to be "engaged in constant skirmishes with the Kandyans in the neighbourhood of Hangwell. The fort at that place is in so ruined a state that he was obliged to take post in the Modeleor's house, which is enclosed by a slight wall. Here he was three times successively attacked by large bodies of the enemy, but defended his station with great ability and resolution . . . On the morning of 5th September a small party marched from Colombo to reinforce the garrison of Hangwell; and, in the evening of the same day, Captain William Pollock, of His Majesty's 51st Regiment, was sent to command the whole detachment, which did not much exceed one hundred men. He rode up, protected only by his own sword and pistols . . .

"Next morning (the 6th, at 10 A.M.) Hangwell was attacked by the grand army of the Kandyans, commanded by the King in person. They advanced with more than usual boldness, firing grape-shot from their artillery, which struck the wall behind which our troops were stationed: the effects of it, however, were not felt. Had balls been used, the consequences would have been more dangerous. Captain Pollock, anxious to bring the Kandyans as near to him as possible, made no attempt to retard their progress. When they had advanced within two hundred yards of the house, and halted as if afraid to come to close quarters, the officer above-mentioned sent a detachment of his troops, under Lieutenant Mercer, through an unseen path in the wood, to enfilade the left flank of the undisciplined multitude. Having allowed time for a co-operation to take effect, he sallied forth with the remainder of his garrison, who were soon in the midst of the enemy. The slaughter from both quarters began almost at the same moment. Resistance continued about two hours, when, the shot of a field-piece reaching near the station of the King, he retreated with precipitation, and was followed by his whole army . . . On our side only two men were wounded on this occasion; but . . . the coolies belonging to the detachment buried two hundred and seventy of them (the enemy) on the day subsequent to the battle . . . The men under the command of Captain Pollock were only convalescents, and all afflicted with weakness in their knees—a complaint universally felt by every person who recovered from Ceylon fever."

The present resthouse is almost surrounded by the old moat of the fort, which is all that remains to recall its past history of heroism.

Mr. H. White, in *The Orientalist*, sums up in a few comprehensive sentences the history of the ancient city of Sitawaka, situated about half-a-mile from Avisawella, on the Yatiyantota road. "The place which, in the 'dark and backward abysm of time' was the jungle fastness to which Sita was carried by Ravan, was, in the middle ages of Ceylon history, the petty fortress where a tributary prince raised the standard of revolt. Sacked and burnt again and again by Sinhalese and Portuguese, it was for a brief period the capital of a *de facto* king.

"The halting-place of English troops and embassies, it became a petty fort again, and is now a small judicial out-station, with a prosaic police court and gaol. The very name Sitawaka has disappeared from modern maps."

In very ancient times the King of Sitawaka was regarded as supreme in the low country, a traditional seniority which he retained for several hundred years, but latterly more as a convention than a practical supremacy. The historical importance of Sitawaka is inseparable from the name of Mayadunne, who was given the kingdom by his brother, the King of Kotte, in 1534. He rebuilt the city on a magnificent scale, and from its shelter proved himself to be a thorn in the side of the Portuguese and a danger to all who were not his allies. It was not only his military prowess that led to his success, but also his crafty diplomacy and masterly conception of the art of bribery; he knew and boasted that his gold was "the best persuader." Sitawaka being large, and built on both sides of the river, was difficult to defend against a powerful force; twice, therefore, when attacked by the Portuguese, Mayadunne retired to his mountain fastnesses, leaving the beds made and the lights burning in the decorated palace, with a tactful message that, as the city was not large enough to hold both himself and his visitors, he had thought best to vacate it during their stay.

King Raja Sinha I., who followed Mayadunne at Sitawaka, nearly succeeded in capturing Colombo, while his very name struck awe into the hearts of the Portuguese. Originally a Buddhist, he became an apostate, and embraced the Hindu religion, since the Hindu priests said that it was possible to expiate his crimes, whereas the Buddhists were sure that in his life he could not do so. To aid his redemption Raja Sinha obtained masons from India and began to build Berendi Kovil, which still stands, restored to something like its former condition; but he never completed the work, although twenty thousand men are said to have worked at it for twenty years, while what was already done was scattered by the Portuguese.

The temple stands at the highest point of a series of three rectangular terraces, approached across a ditch by a bridge, accurately described by Dr. John Davy in 1821 as "composed of large flat stones, each about fifteen feet long, three or four wide, and about two feet thick."

The palace stood on the opposite bank of the river; it, too, was built upon a series of terraces, but, although vast carved stones lie in profusion on its site, all trace of the outline has been lost during the subsequent centuries of military occupation. Near the foot of Kobbotara Gala, a bold cliff that overlooks Sitawaka, lives a family of people called Gala Balanpalage "(The Watchers of the Rock"). Until comparatively recent times some marine birds, probably cormorants, used frequently to fly to this rock, bringing fish with them. It was the duty of the watchers to take the fish from the birds (how this was done is not recorded) and carry it at once to the palace for the Royal table. The birds seem to have become tired of constantly losing their prey, since they no longer come to the rock.

In 1593 Raja Sinha reached the climax of his career and suffered a heavy defeat at the hands of the Portuguese. He did not long survive his reverse. While retiring to Sitawaka from north of Ruwanella a bamboo splinter which ran into his foot caused blood-poisoning, and "the astrologer, Dodampe Ganitaya, by influence of magic, prevented the poison of the wound from being extracted . . . Raja Sinha was brought from Petangoda in the Royal barge (down the Kelaniya and up the Sitawaka *ganga*), and on the way remained silent except at the place called Kukulubitterawella, where, without uttering another word, he expired," on the threshold of his city.

The barge was at once put ashore on the great "*wella*" (sandbank) that still lies in the river at that place, and the king was buried in a "*sohona*" (tomb) on the opposite bank. The *sohona*, half-a-mile beyond Taldua Club, is now marked by two small stones beneath an orange-tree—an insignificant memorial to Ceylon's greatest king.

Kukulubitterawella is the version of the name given in the *Rajawaliya*, but the place is called Kikilibitterawella, probably more correctly, since "Cock's-egg Sandbank" is rather an anomalous title. Opposite to the sandbank there are the remains of deep trenches, said to have been dug by Raja Sinha, in order to form an outpost to Sitawaka. An elderly lady diffidently relates that her husband here dug up some cannon balls, the size of an orange, but as he left her some time ago, apparently taking the cannon balls with him, she does not know where they are—and cares less where he is. Since the subject seemed a painful one politeness forbade further inquiry.

The Portuguese did not use the site of the palace for their fort, as their requirements consisted of a lookout combined with a redoubt, for which high ground was essential. They, therefore, occupied the top of a hill close to the river, known as Belum Kanda ("Lookout Hill"), where a work of nine sides, each thirty-six feet long, was constructed of stone, now buried in thick *chena*, rendering it very difficult of access.

When the Dutch occupied Sitawaka in 1675 they seized upon the terraced site of the palace as affording an excellent series of defensive positions, crowned at the highest point by a strong square fort, built of stone from the ancient ruins. At each terrace a stone "*bemma*" (ramp) was built, with two breastworks leading up to Belum Kanda Fort. The Dutchman, Schweitzer, who was stationed here, gives a description of the fort, which serves also to indicate the habits of the Dutch soldier:

"It is situated upon a rocky ground; near to this, just over the river, stood heretofore the King of Sittawack's palace (Berendi Kovil), ruin'd since by the Portuguese. It (the fort) is about four hundred paces in circuit. It is built four squares, with four Bastions, call'd Rycloff, Louisa, Colombo, and Gala: each of these Bastions hath two pieces of large cannon. In the middle of this place is a large square bulwark: under this are kept the provisions, as rice, flesh, salt, and brandy; and the ammunitions of war, powder, granadoes, and bells. Over that was the guard-room, where all the men lay; at each corner of which were five small pieces of cannon. Half the men might have leave to be out of the Fort in the daytime, but at night they were to be in, every man, upon pain of death. Every night the names were call'd and prayers read; and Sunday night we had a sermon preach'd in the guard-chamber . . . This Fort, besides, serves a guard upon the precious stones, as rubies, saphyrs, emeralds, the topaz, and azure stones, that lie in and upon the ground. They are sometimes washt into the rivers by the great rain and water floods."

The Dutch held the fort for about ten years, abandoning it in 1686. Dr. Davy, when travelling this way, was conducted to this fort, wherein he noticed a deep well, which still exists. He remarks that "the walls which two centuries, at least, had spared, have been pulled down . . . and their stones removed to build a new resthouse," but adds, with his usual profound philosophy, "the curious traveller will complain of this measure; whilst the indolent one will bless his stars for being saved the trouble of forcing his way through thickets to see an old ruin, the materials of which, newly arranged, afford him a comfortable shelter."

On the opposite side of the Getaheta *ela* is the site of a "*hakuru atuwa*" (jaggery barn), commanded by the fire of the fort, where in Sinhalese times, and probably as late as the Dutch period, jaggery was stored for trade purposes. The plateau of land on which the barn stood is surrounded by an "*agala*" (moat), which was filled with water in order to prevent ants from approaching the storehouse. The precaution might seem at first sight an impracticable measure, but its success is attested by the fact that there are several such barns in existence, each surrounded by a similar trench.

The centre of Avisawella has moved to the neighbourhood of the railway station since the time of Davy, when the main town clustered round the hill on which stood the British military cantonment in 1800, now occupied by the Police Magistrate's bungalow.

CHAPTER SIX

"RAMAYANA"

"This noble tale whose lines contain
Lessons of duty, love and gain
I now would fain at length recite,
While good men listen with delight."

ONCE upon a time, before the birth of Christ, an Indian named Valmiki wrote a song; it is perhaps undesirable to enter upon statistical calculations with regard to poetry, but some interest attaches to the length of this poem, the *Ramayana*, which runs to three hundred and forty-seven thousand words, contained in five hundred and thirty cantos. The perusal of such a book is a matter to be approached with considerable determination; however, Mr. R. T. H. Griffith not only read it in Sanskrit, but translated it into rhyming English couplets. There is much that is purely repetitive, but the greater part of the work is both interesting and of great poetical merit. The facinating tale which forms the theme of the poem lends itself to Griffith's method of rendering, but the grandeur of the language is inevitably lost in translation. In the following narrative, the later incidents of which occurred at Sitawaka and Ella, free recourse has been made to Griffith's wonderful version, especially to his descriptive passages, while the action, which Valmiki smothers with laudatory detail, has of necessity been condensed into modern prose.

There was an ancient Indian kingdom called Kosal, a happy realm, with fertile length of fair champaign, and flocks and herds and wealth of grain, of which the capital city was called Ayodhya (Oudh). This royal town was of immense size, filled with a just and happy race, and blessed with troops of children, whose parents were contented with their own possessions nor ever longed for the wealth of their richer friends.

"Right glorious was her royal street;
Where streams allayed the dust and heat.
On level ground in even row
Her houses rose in goodly show.
Terrace and palace, arch and gate,
The queenly city decorate.
There reigned a King of name revered,
To country and to town endeared,
Great Dasaratha, good and sage,
Well read in Scripture's holy page :
Upon his kingdom's weal intent,
Mighty and brave and provident ;
For firm and just and ever true.
Love, duty, gain, he kept in view.
But splendid, just, and great of mind,

The childless King for offspring pined.
No son had he his name to grace,
Transmitter of his royal race.
Long had his anxious bosom wrought
And as he pondered rose the thought:
'A votive steed 'twere good to slay,
So might a son the gift repay.'"

He laid the proposition before his ministers, who were of opinion that the experiment was worth trying, provided that the horse was killed, with the utmost ceremonial, by a Brahman of sufficient social and ecclesiastical eminence. At this juncture Sumantra, an adviser of proven worth, rose to tell a tale of days gone by, how from Dasaratha's ancient line a son should spring.

In the neighbouring kingdom of Angad, a king called Lomapad, by living a life of folly, brought upon the land an unprecedented plague and drought, which lasted for several years. When the King begged his Brahmans to think of some way of checking these calamities, the wisest of them told him that it would be necessary for the Princess Royal to marry the son of a certain very saintly hermit. Now the proposed bridegroom, whose name was Rishyasring, had lived all his life alone with his father in the depths of the forest, where he had never seen another mortal; spending his whole time obedient to the strictest rule that forms a young ascetic's school. The question was, therefore, how to persuade him to leave the life of devotion with his hermit father for the mundane career of a Prince Consort presumptive. Clearly it was useless to ask the boy outright to come and marry the Princess Santa, his whole training would dictate a refusal, but it was felt that if he could be enticed to the Court and meet his bride he would fall a victim to her charms. It was, therefore, decided that a party of damsels, "rich in each charm that wakes desire, with eyes that burn with amorous fire," should be sent to beguile Rishyasring from his forest solitude, during the absence of his father from home. The maidens, disguised as young hermits, so that the recluse should not be unduly startled by their appearance, sailed in ships decked cunningly with leaves, to create the illusion that they were part of the forest. On arrival in the neighbourhood of the hermit's hut they waited until the old man had gone out, then—

> "With bolder steps they ventured nigh
> To catch the youthful hermit's eye,
> And all the damsels, blithe and gay,
> At various games began to play.
> They tossed the flying ball about
> With dance and song and merry shout."

As might be expected, it was not long before young Rishyasring, hearing the laughter, came to the spot, where, after overcoming his initial embarrassment, he soon joined in the sport.

Delighted by the beauty and lively conversation of his new companions, Rishyasring, with unpractised but very creditable hospitality, invited the party of "hermits" to his hut.

> "Then round his neck fair arms were flung,
> And there the laughing damsels clung,
> And pressing nearer and more near,
> With sweet lips whispered at his ear;
> While rounded limb and swelling breast
> The youthful hermit softly pressed."

When the young ladies took their leave, Rishyasring, though puzzled, was quite decided that he would like to see more of them, and arranged a rendezvous for the next day. His father, to whom he related his experiences, opined that the visitors were giants in disguise, and cautioned him to have no more to do with them; but Rishyasring was already "sweetly vanquished," and no sooner was his father out of sight on the following morning than he made quick time to the meeting-place. This time they enticed him on to their ship without the least difficulty—in fact for a novice he displayed a very rapid appreciation of their charms, and, due to their kind treatment, gave no trouble on finding himself kidnapped: probably anticipating that all the inhabitants of Angad resembled his fascinating captors. As the ship put into port, a mighty shower of rain vindicated in part the truth of the ancient prophecy, while

Rishyasring's marriage with the Princess Santa synchronized with the immediate abatement of the plague that had raged for so long.

Sumantra's tale of ancient days left a general consensus of opinion in Dasaratha's Council that, as a slayer of votive steeds, Rishyasring, who still lived at Angad, was the ideal man. A Brahman such as he, so obviously blessed by the gods, would render the success of the sacrifice inevitable. King Dasaratha, therefore, after giving his queens a general outline of the scheme, set forth in great state to fetch Rishyasring, leaving his wives in a tremor of excitement, for all three were as anxious as their lord for a son. Rishyasring, who readily consented to be the principal performer at the sacrifice, returned with Dasaratha to Ayodhya, where immense preparations were in progress for the ceremony.

During the intricate ritual of the sacrifice it occurred to the gods that the birth of a son to Dasaratha might be a suitable opportunity to dispose of an irritating giant named Ravan, who ruled a vast host of "*rakshas*" (demons) in Lanka (Ceylon). At one time Ravan spent ten thousand years in dire austerities, finishing with an offering of all his heads to Brahma, who, impressed by this devotion, decreed that his death should not be encompassed save by human agency. After this reward Ravan became quite uncontrollable, spurning the bonds of law, turning his fancy to others' wives, marring the holy rites of Brahmans, and indulging in every form of breach of the peace, confident that he was much too big for any mortal yet born to kill, and secure in the knowledge that no god could harm him.

The Lord Vishnu consented, at the request of the assembled gods, to materialize himself in fourfold mortal form, as the four sons whom the gods were about to vouchsafe to Dasaratha. This undertaking, which facilitated the fulfilment of the King's sacrificial prayers, also provided an opportunity for the god to bring about Ravan's death through the mortal agency of one of the young princes in whom his spirit was to be incorporated. Vishnu's first step was to appear in the flame of Dasaratha's equine sacrifice as a vast figure of awful might, dark, robed in red, and bearing a vase of nectar, which a drumlike voice, loud and low, directed Dasaratha to give to his fair wives. The King was filled with rapture :

> " Quick to the ladies' bower he sped,
> And there to Queen Kausalya said,
> ' This genial nectar take and quaff,'
> He spoke and gave the lady half."

Then, after dividing the remainder between Sumitra and Kaikeyi, his other two queens, he settled down to await developments. He was not long in suspense, for " soon with rapture and with pride each Royal Dame conceived "— a conclusion to his sacrificial efforts that caused the monarch transports of joy, during which "he gazed upon each lady's face and triumphed as he gazed."

After Rishyasring's return to Angad the months flew by, until at last Ayodhya was filled with such a riot of rejoicing as had never before been seen within its blissful walls. Queen Kausalya, at a most auspicious moment, gave birth to a son, who was named Rama: next Queen Kaikeyi bore a son called Bharat, then Sumitra had twins, Laksman and Satrughna. Dasaratha was delighted at the generosity of the gods, who had thus provided him, in minimum time, with a presentable family of boys. Even Sumitra's twins were welcome, although Rama, the first heir, who represented half of Vishnu, was the father's favourite.

Rama grew up into a youth of prodigious qualities; in learning, sport or warlike arts he not only beat other boys of his age, but excelled grown men of proven experience. The brothers, as is often the case, formed special attachments within the family, Rama and Laksman being inseparable, while Bharat and Satrughna were seldom seen apart. All four were devotedly attached to one another, but the three juniors acknowledged Rama as their leader, both on account of seniority and character.

A contemporary king called Janak had such a wondrously beautiful and accomplished daughter that he was much concerned as to how he should make sure of a suitable husband for her. He decided eventually that a good criterion would be the power to string the mighty bow of Siva, which was in his possession. This was such a stiff test that it began to seem as if the fair Sita might be an old maid, until Rama, attracted by the lady's charms, tried his hand, and not only affixed the bowstring, but drew the bow until it broke. After this demonstration of his prowess, Janak handed over Sita with no more comment than is contained in four ordinary cantos, much to the delight of the girl herself, who had been considerably attracted by her handsome suitor. Sita, although appropriated in her infancy as his daughter by Janak, in reality sprang from a furrow turned by that monarch as he was ploughing his fields. Perhaps due in part to her miraculous origin, her figure was divinely proportioned, with broad hips and slender waist; while her legs, if it is permissible to discuss these members, were "long and neat, and somewhat long her dainty feet." Her face must have been beyond the power of Valmiki to portray, or he would have devoted a few words to it, but her eyes, "pure as the moon of autumn skies," were long, and so dark that she is frequently described as "The lady of the large black eye."

Naturally, at a period when India was overrun by giants and demons, a young man of Rama's abilities was in much demand to curtail the careers of these unpleasant monsters, who, with unmerciful persistency, harassed the numerous saints and hermits then living in the forest.

King Dasaratha, who was getting old, and wished to retire, decided, after prolonged consideration, to hand over the kingdom to his eventual successor, Rama—a course of procedure which the young man's attributes rendered eminently practical. Without being in any way a prig, Rama displayed a plethora of virtues which it is unnecessary to enumerate, since they form a complete list of all the good qualities known to mankind. Faults he had none.

Up to this point in the story the action has merely provided a setting for the preliminary genealogy, but now the real plot begins.

Queen Kaikeyi, the mother of Bharat, employed a humpbacked handmaiden called Manthara, who had served her since both were children. This maiden, hearing of King Dasaratha's intention to place Rama upon the throne, was so consumed with rage at the prospect of her beloved mistress's son taking a definite second place that her eyeballs turned red and sin burned in her breast. She sped to the queen, and with subtlety worked upon her susceptibilities until Kaikeyi felt that she was really aggrieved; then with treacherous art the humpback reminded her mistress of a promise which King Dasaratha had once made to her, that on two separate occasions whatever she chose to ask should be granted. These boons were intended as an expression of gratitude for her services in rescuing him, grievously wounded, from the field of battle between the gods and demons, and for her solicitude in nursing him back to health; but she had not hitherto demanded the redemption of the promise.

Acting upon Manthara's advice, Kaikeyi, having disordered her robes and hair, retired to a small, dark, unfurnished room, maintained for the use of the King's wives when they were sulky, and aptly called by Griffith "the growlery." Here King Dasaratha, consumed with love, "his lady lying on the ground, in most unqueenly posture found." The King, distressed at his favourite's seeming melancholy, not only fell into the trap laid for him by the scheming woman, but enmeshed himself still further by swearing another mighty oath to fulfil any boon she cared to ask. Then she sprang upon him the request that her son Bharat should be put upon the throne, in place of Kausalya's son Rama, and that Rama should be banished as a hermit for fourteen years to the impenetrable forest of Dandak.

The shock was so great that the poor man "fell prone as falls a smitten tree," murmuring incoherently of the anguish which the fulfilment of his promise would mean to him; but Kaikeyi was adamant, and, after an interminable amount of argument, Dasaratha found himself compelled to banish his favourite son and heir to the jungle. Rama's wife and brother then rallied round with estimable loyalty, Sita refusing to be dissuaded from her purpose of accompanying her husband into exile, and, when he made known his intention of joining them, no one daring to argue with Laksman, who was second only to Rama in prowess. Even Rama, though delighted at his wife's fidelity, was a little doubtful of her capacity to withstand the rigours of forest life, where, besides the lack of all domestic amenities,

> "'Tis hard to ford each treacherous flood
> So thick with crocodiles and mud."

But Sita's resolution was unshakable, and she had her way. As far as can be gathered no one, except Kaikeyi and Manthara, was pleased at Rama's banishment; most of the population of Ayodhya accompanied the exiles upon the first part of their journey to Dandak, where, after giving them time to settle in a neat thatched hut, Bharat paid a visit, to express his sorrow for the part which he was forced to play by the unwelcome turn of events. Rama, who bore him no ill will, entreated him to keep the kingdom in good order until the fourteen years were over.

In the forest Rama and Laksman had most exciting adventures, slaying so many giants and giantesses that at last the whole remaining tribe of Dandak monsters, headed by one Khara, advanced upon the devoted couple. Nothing daunted, the heroes gave battle to the monstrous host, from which Akampan, the only giant who escaped, fled to Lanka, where he told the dreaded Ravan of the slaughter of his friends and relatives in Dandak.

A short description of Ravan will give some idea of Rama's new enemy. The giant, who was in stature like a mountain height, possessed twenty arms and ten heads; his mouths gaped wide at every breath, which seems to indicate that he had adenoids in all ten noses, and his huge frame, resembling lazulite, adorned with gold, was covered with healed wounds, incurred during his endless incursions upon the private property both of gods and men. Acknowledging that it would be impossible even for Ravan, with his army of demons, to defeat Rama and Laksman in open warfare, Akampan suggested a foul plot to Ravan, whetting his appetite the while with a description of Sita's attractions.

"His wife, above all women graced,
Is Sita, of the dainty waist,
With limbs to fair proportion true,
And a soft skin of lustrous hue.
Round neck and arm rich gems are twined:
She is the gem of womenkind.
And none to rival her would dare
'Mid dames who part the long black hair.
That hero in the wood beguile,
And steal his lovely spouse the while.
'Reft of his darling wife, be sure,
Brief days the mourner will endure."

This was exactly the type of predatory

expedition in which Ravan, by long practice, had become expert ; so, mounting into his flying car, he sailed over from Lanka to engage the services of a fiend called Marichcha, who could be trusted to carry out the beguiling strategy with unrivalled skill. To Ravan's surprise and annoyance Marichcha counselled him to give up the enterprise, as any interference with Rama would lead only to trouble for the whole of Lanka, besides probably resulting in his own downfall.

Reluctantly Ravan abandoned the plan, but on returning to his palace in the city of Lanka he was met by a giantess named Suranakha, who, having seen the "plain, spread with the fourteen thousand slain," had fled, like Akampan, to bear the news to Ravan. She was easily able to rouse the Lord of Lanka to such a pitch of rage that he returned at once to Marichcha. This fiend he compelled to undertake the task of straying, in the form of a beautiful deer, marked with silver spots, near the hut where Rama and Sita lived. It was an ingenious plan, relying for its success upon the practical certainty that, at Sita's request, Rama would pursue the unusually marked animal, leaving Laksman to guard his wife. When he had led his pursuer deep into the jungle Marichcha was to cry out to Laksman for help, imitating Rama's voice; then if, as in all probability would happen, Laksman dashed away to help his brother, Ravan, in the guise of a mendicant,

" OH ! COME THIS GLORIOUS CREATURE SEE "

would approach Sita and carry her off to Lanka.

The scheme succeeded perfectly; Sita, while gathering flowers, saw the deer gleaming like gold, and called to her husband to come and see it.

> "Again, again, she called in glee,
> 'Oh! come this glorious creature see:
> Quick, quick, my Lord, this deer to view,
> And bring thy brother Laksman, too.'"

Such was her rapture that Rama could do nothing less than try to catch it for her, although Laksman, with damping caution, advised leaving it alone, and was accordingly snubbed as being a wet blanket.

Marichcha, although killed in the hunt, accomplished his vocal imitation of Rama with his dying breath to such good effect that, after a heated argument with Sita, Laksman was unwillingly driven forth by the anxious wife to render aid, if necessary, to her husband. Ravan took his chance, and within a few minutes Sita, almost entirely through her own fault in not listening to the cautious Laksman, was travelling rapidly towards Lanka as a captive in the giant's air-car, after refusing his coarse suggestion that she should accompany him willingly. It is not to be supposed that Sita went quietly —quite the reverse—she screamed and shrieked with such vigour that she woke an old vulture called Jayatus, who was asleep on a lofty tree.

This old bird disapproved so strongly of Ravan's dastardly act of abduction that, in spite of their disparity in age, he challenged the comparatively youthful giant to mortal combat, in an attempt to rescue Sita. Unfortunately, after a terrific fight, in which Jayatus completely wrecked the air-car, Ravan's youth told, and the vulture was left to die, game to the very last moment. Ravan then had to propel himself through the air, on foot, as it were, with Sita tucked under his arm, an undignified position, which she strongly resented.

After crossing the sea, Sinhalese tradition maintains, Ravan left Sita to rest for a short time in a large cave near Ella, before taking her on to his capital, which was situated where the ruins of Sitawaka now lie. The cave at Ella is situated on the western side of the valley that opens out upon the low country. It is a difficult climb to its mouth, and inside the cavern, which is full of bats, a ladder is necessary to negotiate the descent to floor-level, where the way is blocked by a large pool of water. Beyond this pool is said to stretch a labyrinth of passageways, in which the explorer is soon lost, never to emerge.

On arrival at Sitawaka, Ravan placed Sita under the care of several very unhandsome giantesses, in a delightful grove of Asoka trees, where every luxury she could desire was offered for her delectation. Her peace of mind, however, was not increased by the behaviour of her captor, who alternated passionate wooing with bloody threats, at one moment entreating her love :

> " One word of grace, one look I crave ;
> Have pity on thy postrate slave,"

but the next instant warning her of a fearful fate if she continued to flout him :

> " Two months, fair dame, I grant thee still,
> To bend thee to thy lover's will,
> If when that respite time be fled
> Thou still refuse to share my bed
> My cooks shall mince they flesh with steel
> And serve it for my morning meal."

Ravan was restrained from forcible attainment of his desires by a dreadful curse laid upon him many years before. Meeting Punjikasthala, the beautiful daughter of King Varun, on her way to the palace of Brahma, he had, with dastardly violence, compelled her to his pleasure before allowing her to flee ravished to the feet of the lord of heaven, who, indignant at the crime, adjured the giant as follows:

> " If, Ravan, thou a second time,
> Be guilty of so foul a crime,
> Thy heads in shivers shall be rent,
> Be warned, and dread the punishment."

Rama and Laksman meanwhile, after some acrimonious recriminations, organized an energetic search, which Rama was determined not to relinquish until his faithful wife was found. Luckily they came across Jayatus, who, not quite dead even yet, explained the mystery of Sita's disappearance before drawing his final breath. After further adventures with giants and hermits Rama eventually entered into an alliance with Sugriva, who, till lately King of the Vanars, or monkey people, had been turned off his throne and exiled with a few faithful ministers by his brother, Bali. Sugriva had cause to be aggrieved. He had waited for a whole year outside a cave into which his elder brother, Bali, had gone to kill a fiend, then assuming that the fiend had won he blocked up the cave, to prevent the creature's escape, and took over the government. But Bali, who turned up later, having taken rather longer than he expected to kill the monster, refused to believe that Sugriva had not blocked him in on purpose as soon as he was safely inside. Unpleasantness ensued, which resulted in Sugriva's banishment to the jungle, where, smarting under his recent mortification, he readily espoused Rama's cause, on condition that assistance should first be given him to recover the lost Vanar throne. Bali was slain by Rama without undue difficulty, leaving Sugriva in an excellent position, as sovereign of the realm, to assemble a vast army of Vanars for the invasion of Lanka. There was a little delay to begin with, owing to Sugriva's over-indulgence in the pleasures of his newly restored Court and his infatuation for his deceased brother's wife, a union not regarded with any disapproval in those days.

The Chief Minister of Sugriva was Hanuman, an accomplished Vanar, who could change his form, either in size or appearance, at a moment's notice, besides being able to travel in prodigious leaps through the air for vast distances, a mobility which he perhaps inherited from his father, the Wind God. This deity, attracted by an extremely pretty nymph alone upon a hill, took a somewhat unfair advantage of his invisibility, but the lady, after learning the identity of her unseen and unexpected lover, was intensely gratified when little Hanuman was born.

While Sugriva tarried, Hanuman, taking Rama's ring as a token, set off with a few companions to make a reconnaissance of Lanka, and, if possible, to rescue Sita, without the complications of an organized invasion of Ravan's territory. On reaching the straits that separate Ceylon from India the question arose among the little company of monkeys as to whether Hanuman could jump across; whereupon, to prove his ability, the Vanar not only leapt the sea, but rose to the heights of heaven in doing so, thereby incurring a certain amount of jealous envy among the serpentine inhabitants of that sphere. Landing in Lanka Hanuman hastened immediately towards Ravan's city, which so entranced him with its beauty at first sight that he paused a while to view it.

Stately domes and tall turrets, rising from within an encircling golden wall, were shaded by palms and myraid fruit-trees, whose delicious loads hung down to the noble streets; while sweet birds sang in the scented groves, among sparkling fountains and translucent ponds, where gorgeous water-fowl played around the floating lotuses.

Being a rather conspicuous figure in his normal proportions, the Vanar dwarfed himself to the size of a cat before entering the city by moon light, but nevertheless the Guardian Goddess of Lanka, who noticed the entry of an enemy, met him upon the ramparts with a demand for an explanation of his purpose. As Hanuman's account of himself was unsatisfactory she struck him on the throat, whereat in a fury he knocked her down, before realizing his ungallant act in handling a lady so roughly. However, the cave-man attitude had an excellent effect, since the goddess submitted immediately, recognizing Hanuman as the destroyer of Lanka, whose coming had been prophesied by Brahma. Provided that he did not attract the attention of the inhabitants, the city was now open for the search which Hanuman had come to make, so he began an exhaustive exploration of every building wherein it was possible that Sita might be concealed. During the course of his investigations Hanuman came upon many scenes which pleased him immensely, but none more so than the great hall where Ravan lay asleep after an exceedingly indulgent banquet, surrounded by bevies of girls whose beauty exceeded even that of the ladies of Sugriva's Court, where taste ran as high as was then thought possible:

"'Tis Indra's heaven,' the Vanar cried,
Gazing in joy from side to side;
'The home of all the gods is this,
The mansion of eternal bliss.'
There were the softest carpets spread,
Delightful to the sight and tread,
Where many a lovely woman lay,
O'ercome by sleep, fatigued with play;
The wine no longer cheered the feast,
The sound of revelry had ceased.
With wondering eyes a while he viewed
Each graceful form and attitude;
One lady's head was backward thrown,
Bare was her arm and loose her zone.
There slept another whose small hand
Had loosened every tie and band.
In careless grace another lay
With gems and jewels cast away.
Another black-eyed damsel pressed
Her lute upon her heaving breast,
As though her loving arms were twined
Round him for whom her bosom pined,
The while her long soft hair concealed
The beauties that her friend revealed.
With limbs at random interlaced
Round arm and leg and throat and waist,
That wreath of women lay asleep,
Like blossoms in a careless heap."

Remarking, with the eye of a connoisseur, that Mandodari, lying by Ravan's side, was even more beautiful than the rest, Hanuman was at first inclined to think that she might be Sita, whom he had never seen, but soon spurning the thought that Rama's wife would be so unfaithful, he dragged himself away from the entrancing spectacle to continue his search. After having closely examined almost every sleeping lady in Lanka—a task which he did not find displeasing—Hanuman was in despair at not discovering Sita, until, observing an Asoka grove still unsearched, he leapt the wall and climbed a tree, from which commanding position he saw the object of his adventure:

" Fair as Kailasa white with snow
He saw a palace flash and glow,
Where, pallid, with neglected dress,
Watched close by fiend and giantess,
Her sweet face thin with constant flow
Of tears, with fasting and with woe,
From her dear friends and husband torn,
Amid the cruel fiends forlorn,
Who fierce-eyed watch around her kept,
A tender woman sat and wept.
Her sobs, her sighs, her mournful mien,
Her glorious eyes, proclaimed the Queen.
' This, this, is she,' the Vanar cried,
' Fair as the moon and lotus-eyed.' "

Hanuman, although he had now a complete knowledge of the geography of Ravan's city, would not leave without making an effort to console the captive queen. He did not expect her, after her recent experiences, to trust him so far as to allow of his carrying her away, but at least it was in his power to give her news of the prospective invasion that would secure her release. Approaching Sita very slowly, he began a valedictory monologue upon the virtues of Rama, until, her attention attracted, the lady raised her eyes and almost roused the sleeping fiends in her terror at the monkey that stood before her. At length, however, with the aid of Rama's ring, Hanuman was able to soothe her fears, and to persuade her of his genuine helpful purpose. As he expected, she refused to accept his offer to carry her back to India, partly because she would not voluntarily allow her limbs to touch those of anyone but her husband, and partly because she was sure that she would fall from his arms through giddiness at the height of one of his tremendous leaps. Giving Hanuman a gem from her hair, to take as a token to Rama, with ardent messages of love and urgent pleadings for rescue, she pressed him to hasten back to her husband.

There are said to be four expedients to conquer an enemy or make him come to terms: conciliation, gifts, dissension, and force or punishment. Seeing that none of the first would be of any avail, Hanuman decided to commit a little "frightfulness" before leaving. He, therefore, summarily laid waste Ravan's entire pleasure grounds, then, when the awakened giants congregated to inquire the meaning of this devastation, defied them all, and fought until he was overpowered and captured. Having bound him, the giants decided to burn off his tail before sending him back to Rama as an example of the fate that awaited spies in Lanka. They, therefore, wrapped his caudal appendage in oil-soaked cloths and set it alight. "The tail, I fancy, is the part," said King Ravan, "most cherished by a monkey's heart." Although, at Sita's prayer, the fire refused to do more than singe his tail, Hanuman, annoyed by the smarting insult, reduced himself to his minutest size and stepped out of his bonds, then, having resumed his normal proportions, with the cloths still alight, he ran about all over the city, spreading conflagration wherever he went. After this escapade he returned to the mainland, where he delighted Rama with the glad news that his wife was still safe.

The huge Vanar army of monkeys and bears that had now collected was forthwith put on the march towards the straits that separate Lanka from India, led by Sugriva, who was confident in the ability of his monkeys to overcome every obstacle in their path. When the news of this advance reached Ravan he encouraged his chiefs with supreme assurance, like a modern boxing champion before a fight: "Tell them that I was never in better condition in my life, and am confident of success." But a sage old giant named Vibishan, the brother of Ravan, who had guessed the divine purpose which Rama was sent to fulfil, counselled the King, in the height of his boastful declamations, to give up Sita and avoid the certain destruction that her retention would bring upon the entire kingdom. Ravan would not listen, and was so furious at such a suggestion that he kicked the unfortunate Vibishan off his seat—an insult that caused the old giant's desertion to the ranks of Rama.

By this time the Vanar army had reached the shores of Southern India, where its size and warlike efficiency were viewed with alarm by Ravan's spies. An attempt was made to seduce Sugriva from Rama's side by promises of power and wealth, but the Vanar king flouted the suggestion with the contempt that such a sign of weakness deserved. In the meantime, with dogged persistency, the monkeys began to build a bridge across the seas that separated them from Lanka—a hostile act for which Ravan tried to take revenge by a despicable attempt at undermining Sita's faithfulness. He caused Vidyujjhva, a magician of vast cunning, to make a perfect model of Rama's head, which he showed to Sita, assuring her that now her husband was slain she no longer had cause to refuse his amorous advances. The ruse was a failure in so far as Ravan's object was concerned, since, although Sita was completely deceived, her relentless attitude towards the giant was, if possible, strengthened by this outrage. The captive's anguish at the supposed news of her husband's death was at length solaced by one of her fiendish wardresses, who, taking pity on the moaning woman, was in the act of relating the true circumstances of the case when the first sounds of Rama's approaching army were heard in the city.

During a reconnaissance of the defences of the fortress from a hill, Sugriva, espying Ravan on the top of a high turret, leapt to the place and engaged the giant in a desperate single combat, but, finding himself by no means successful, escaped—we will not say fled—with a higher respect of his antagonist than he had hitherto held.

After this the Vanars methodically invested the city and settled down to the monotony of a siege, which was punctuated throughout by heroic combats between the leading chieftains on either side. Rama and Laksman were at last pitted against enemies worthy of their prowess; Indrajit, Ravan's son, pierced them both with arrows which induced a trance, so that the Vanar army thought them dead. But Vibishan knew the secret of the poison, and, urging Sugriva to lead the battle, posted guards around the mighty pair until at last they awoke furious at the indignity they had suffered. Ravan, with commendable military skill, reserved himself until his foes were becoming tired by their exertions, then suddenly sallied forth at the head of the pick of his troops, to hurl himself upon the war-worn besiegers. The Vanars, however, staunch to a monkey, awaited the onslaught, and, armed with huge rocks and tree-stems, eventually repulsed the counter-attack with enormous loss. Ravan, seriously alarmed at this defeat, decided to awake his mightiest giant, called Kumbhakarna, who was in the habit of sleeping for six months at a time, with intervals of one day for food and drink—a restriction placed upon him by Brahma, lest he should destroy the whole world. The emissaries who were sent upon the dangerous task of calling him departed with huge loads of raw meat and other delicacies, in order to appease the monster in his wrath at being suddenly awakened. But the rousing of the sleeper proved to be an extremely difficult business. He was entirely indifferent to their shouting, which was like thunder, and to the noise of cymbals, conches, neighing horses and trumpeting elephants, in such volumes of sound that the birds fell dead from concussion. They drenched him with water, beat him on the face with maces, and dropped large fragments of rock upon him, but it was not until elephants trod upon his chest and head that the unusual weight awoke him. He was rather cross, but after a heavy meal consented to hear an explanation of the unprecedented departure that had been followed in waking him after only a couple of months. Realizing at last that the city was aotually in danger, he strode to the scene of action, licking his lips at the prospect of a feast of monkeys and bears.

It has to be admitted that his presence, towering above the walls of Lanka before he made his sally, inspired among the Vanars much the same emotions as a tank does among infantrymen, but they stood up to him in all their thousands, hampering his activities against their leaders by their constant attacks. The most desperate struggle of the siege ensued, in which, after thousands of Vanars had fallen, Rama at length decapitated Kumbhakarna with an arrow from the quiver of the Lord Indra, Chief of the Gods.

It might be thought that this reverse would bring about the capitulation of Lanka, but Ravan was not conquered until he was killed. Once more, after an elaborate sacrifice, Indrajit, the magician, took the field, where he was so successful that he slew not only Rama and Laksman, but bears and monkeys in monstrous piles, including all their leaders except Hanuman and Vibishan. These two, searching sorrowfully among the dead for the bodies of the two heroes, came upon Jambavan, the Bear-King, sorely wounded, who told Hanuman where, beyond the Himalayas, was a mountain on which grew herbs that would restore life to the slain. The Vanar, exerting to the utmost his marvellous mobility, returned while it was yet night with the herbs, of which the wondrous fragrance, penetrating throughout the entire battlefield, restored life to the thousands of Indrajit's victims, so that before dawn they delivered an overpowering night-attack, in which the city was set on fire.

Indrajit came forth again, bearing in his chariot a magic image of Sita, which he cut down with his sword in sight of the infuriated Rama; but Laksman, rendered invincible by anger, broke the chariot in pieces and slew the magician, while Ravan's mightiest warriors fell on every hand before the irresistible Vanars. Then at last Ravan himself, having no further resources at his command, again took the field, to fall pierced to the heart by an arrow from Rama's all-conquering bow.

With the fall of Ravan the city surrendered, leaving Rama at liberty to regain his long-lost wife. Declaring Vibishan King of Lanka, in place of his dead brother, Rama ordered Hanuman to bring Sita before him. Timidly, and trembling before the eyes of the myriad gazing Vanars, the faithful lady came to the side of her husband. It is now that, if criticism of a national hero may be permitted, Rama's behaviour appears cruel in the extreme. Knowing, as he must have done, in his heart that she had been unswervingly faithful, he turned to the adoring woman, who had endured such misery in order to retain her purity, and said:

" ' 'Twas not for thee our blood was shed,
Or Lanka filled with quiet dead.

No fond affection for my wife
Inspired me in the hour of strife.
I battled to avenge the cause
Of honour, and insulted laws.
My love is fled, for on thy fame
Lies the dark blot of sin and shame.
The world is all before thee: flee;
Go where thou wilt, but not with me.
How should my home receive again
A mistress soiled with deathless stain?'"

Sita, struck with indignation, even through her passionate grief managed to answer this ungallant address in a few words that plumbed the full depths of Rama's injustice. Having summarily exposed his unprincely conduct in publicly insulting her, she questioned the grounds of his assertion that she had been polluted by Ravan; asked why he had sent messages of endearment by Hanuman; and reminded him of her devotion in following him to the jungle when he was banished. Turning to Laksman, who whole-heartedly supported her, she ordered him to prepare a fire:

"Then, raising suppliant hands, the dame
Prayed humbly to the Lord of Flame:
'As this fond heart, by virtue swayed,
From wifely vows has never strayed,
So universal witness, Fire,
Protect my body on the pyre.'
She ceased: and fearless to the last,
Within the flame's wild fury passed."

This act of cold-blooded courage earned its reward. The Lord of Fire himself brought Sita forth unharmed from the flames, and placing her, adorned with gems and fair raiment, beside her husband publicly proclaimed her purity. Then at last Rama clasped his wife in a fond embrace, which she, displaying still further nobility in her forgiveness of his slur, ardently returned.

After the reunion celebrations were over, the vast army, in glorious array, marched to Ayodhya, where, with due pomp, Rama, now freed from the sentence of banishment by virtue of his glorious career, mounted the throne of Dasaratha, which was willingly vacated by Bharat. Here Valmiki's poem leaves the happy pair to reign in perfect peace over a realm of prosperous citizens:

> "The earth her kindly fruits supplied,
> No harvest failed, no children died,
> Unknown were want, disease and crime:
> So calm, so happy was the time."

An unpleasant sequel, not written by Valmiki, shows Rama in his worst light. Even after the passage of years slanderous tongues, deprecating his folly in taking back Sita as his wife, murmured that it was impossible for her to have escaped unpolluted from the clutches of Ravan. Rama, unable to bear the imputed scandal, although knowing full well her purity and love of him, banished Sita for ever from his presence, to the banks of the Ganges, where Madhari, the Goddess of the Earth, transported her on a divine throne to peace in the kingdom of Hades.

CHAPTER SEVEN

SABARAGAMUWA

A YOUNG man, resting at the foot of a tree during a hunting expedition, saw a hare approaching, pursued by a jackal, but when the hare came near him it turned and chased the jackal, which fled in panic. Then the young man thought: "This is indeed a most propitious place; one day I will build a house here." His prophecy came true when, after attaining the rank of Adigar, as a reward for his services to the British Government, he founded the Mahawalatenna Walauwa. The old one-storeyed building, necessitating a staff of sixty servants, recruited from among the feudal tenants, covered at one time two acres of land. Through the thick walls low, massive doorways led, along a maze of passages, into dimly lighted rooms and small secluded courts, to which admission, except for members of the family, was not only forbidden but impossible. The main centre of activity in an old-fashioned "*walauwa*" (Ceylon mansion) was the "*meda-midula*" (a large square court), usually near the centre of the building, surrounded by a deep cool verandah. Three sides of this open square gave on to the residing and guest rooms, while the fourth was formed by the front of the servants' quarters. Here the "*kumarihamy*." (mistress), sitting on a chair, could direct the energies of her entire household, like a policeman controlling traffic in Piccadilly Circus. As each domestic task was finished the responsible servant reported its completion to the mistress, from whom fresh orders were received; and very seldom did an overlong absence upon any duty pass unreproved.

In the verandah at one corner of the square was an immense rack, about four feet from the floor, upon which, in bags made of rush matting, was stored a vast accumulation of paddy Every evening a wood fire was lighted below this stack of grain, so that the smoke curled up among the massed bags, of which the bottom layer became charred and blackened. This method of storage is still acknowledged to be the best possible treatment of paddy, which, saved by its husk from being smoked, is thus kept dry and free from the molestations of animals and insects. Before this fire in the evenings the master of the house installed himself, at home to his guests, while the more junior members of the household and the servants sat round at a respectful distance in reverential groups. Often until midnight the conclave was maintained, with desultory conversation, when, amid the obsequious obeisances of those of his staff still on duty, the old man repaired to his sleeping-chamber with condescending grunts of acknowledgment.

At daybreak he was out again, superintending the duties of his estate, receiving the tithes and presents of his tenants, and controlling the large community over which he exercised a benevolent despotism. In a side verandah of the *walauwa* stood a pair of stocks, frequently occupied by an ill-behaved villager or refractory tenant. Since the prisoners were usually plentifully, although surreptitiously, supplied with food by sympathizers among the household staff, this form of punishment, in spite of its degrading character, was not always regarded with the horror that might have been expected.

The old bakery at Mahawalatenna is entered by a door made of one piece of wood, swinging in the ancient Kandyan style upon pegs, called "*wataw*," left when the door was cut, at the top and bottom of its hinging edge, which is rounded. These pegs were fitted into the transoms when the door was built, so that the breaking of a *watawwa* in a Kandyan house must have been a serious domestic catastrophe, since it would be necessary to take down that part of the wall to refit the door.

The ruins of the ancestral *walauwas* of Ceylon could tell many a story: of political schemes in the chieftain's sanctum; of private intrigue in dim recesses of the gloomy rooms; and of romance in the cool secluded courts, where young lovers spent hours in the silver moonlight. Modern conditions, militating against this semi-feudal system, have rendered impossible the upkeep of the necessary staff to maintain such an establishment, resulting in the dilapidation of most of the old buildings, wherein the owners, as a rule, now occupy only small portions of the one-time extensive mansions.

In a sideroom of the Mahawalatenna Walauwa is a library, stocked with a miscellany of books which demonstrate the extensive intellectual scope of the late owner. On the same shelf can be seen *Fifteen Decisive Battles of the World*; *Psychology, Physical and Moral*; *The Care of Fox Terriers*; Thomas Hardy's novels, and Thurston's *Castes and Tribes of Southern India*: for the book-lover of varied tastes the room is a paradise. In the garden are evidences of other interests—there were at one time sixty kinds of shoe-flowers and eighty varieties of caladiums, but these have suffered very severely from the depredations of a herd of deer.

A Seychelle Islands coconut-palm is growing among its Ceylon relations, but at twenty-three years of age its "crown" has not yet risen above ground-level; it is said that no fruit can be expected until sixty years from the time when it was planted. Every tree in the grounds is either an unusually fine specimen of a common sort, or an example of a species whose peculiar virtues testify to the minute knowledge of his own country which characterized the late chieftain.

Around the *walauwa* are still to be found human testimony of its departed magnificence: old people, born to serve, who certainly have lived for the family and would probably, if necessary, die for it. They exist in the past, their memories peopled with the deeds and sentiments of bygone chiefs, who thought and lived on a lavish, despotic scale, that staggers modern democratic imagination. After crossing the ancient moat the path leads past a piece of land known as the "*bola pittaniya*" (ball-field or, in other words, the cricket ground). Here, when the Ratemahatmaya was batting at the practice nets, his tenants retrieved the balls; a recollection still vivid in the minds of several of the villagers, since "the balls, though small, were very hard when they struck the body."

Sabaragamuwa is rich in archaeological interest, ranging from the ruins of prehistoric cities to the broken walls of Portuguese, Dutch and British forts, but its architectural attractions, though interesting, serve only as a setting for the gems of Kandyan folklore and humour. It is not necessary to delve very deeply into the past to unearth stories which, even if something of their native wit is lost in the absence of a Kandyan raconteur, retain in print a quaint conceit which characterizes the genius of a laughter-loving people. At Galegama, near

Balangoda, there used to be a delightful old "*arachchi*" (headman), who went by the nickname of "Bohoma Hondai Arachchi," on account of his habit of expressing approval of any proposition that pleased him in that amiable phrase, "*Bohoma hondai*" ("Very good"). He once went out shooting with the Government Agent of the province, taking as his weapon an ancient single-barrelled muzzle-loader. In such company the old man wished to be sure of killing his game, so he took great trouble over the loading. Three times he measured out charges of blasting-powder, tamping them down one above the other, and murmuring as each successive charge went in, "*Bohoma hondai*"; then a few more grains of powder for luck, "*Bohooma hondai*"; then some nail-heads, "*Bohoooma hondai,*" and he was ready for anything from a snipe to an elephant. Crossing some open grassland a quail got up; there was a terrible explosion and the *arachchi* was nowhere to be seen. Rushing to the spot the Government Agent and the beaters found the gun in pieces and the old man senseless, but after a time he came round, rather shocked but not dangerously injured. "*Arachchi-rala,*" said one of the beaters, holding out a small mangled bird, "you have been some time without your senses, but here is your quail." A faint smile lit the features of the old headman as he answered faintly: "*Bohoooooma hondai.*"

Stories of an older period are those which centre round the Sinhalese kings and their autocratic rule. One day the King of Kandy, accompanied by his four most eminent ministers, went for a walk round Kandy Lake. While leaning over the wall, discussing affairs of state, or possibly feeding the turtles, His Majesty slipped and fell into the water. At this place the lake was very deep, and the King could not swim, so that he was in imminent danger of drowning. All four of his companions were accomplished swimmers. Two of the ministers expressed acute horror and distress at their monarch's predicament, but otherwise did nothing; the other two gallantly plunged into his assistance and helped him ashore, where he presented a rather undignified spectacle, as is not unusual after unintentional immersion.

His Majesty, in order to avoid a chill, and to escape from the discreetly veiled amusement of his subjects, hurried home to the palace to change. Then he sent for the four ministers.

To the two who had merely expressed consternation he said: "Why, when you can both swim, did you not jump in to save Us?"

"Because," they replied, "the Person of the King is sacred; if we had rescued Your Majesty we should have incurred the death penalty for touching Your Royal Body."

On the face of it this appears to be a valid legal argument, but the King, taking an equitable view, replied: "Our life is more valuable than the lives of you both; you should have sacrificed yourselves and saved Us; virtually you have permitted your King to die when you had means in your power to prevent that catastrophe. We sentence you both to be executed."

The King then addressed the two ministers who had saved him. "What cause have you to show," said he, "why you should not be executed for presuming to touch the Royal Person?"

"Sire," replied they, "had we not done so, Your Highness would have been drowned."

"Your gallantry," replied the King, "is admirable, but it is a well-known legal maxim that hard cases make bad law; besides which, if you are absolved from the penalty for touching Our Person, your action in saving Us loses its merit. We sentence you both to be executed."

Thus by his ingenious acumen was this intelligent monarch rid of four most powerful men.

It is improbable that Ratnapura has ever been mentioned in a book without allusion to its gems; following this precedent, Ribeirio says that there was a headman known as the "Vidana Das Agras" ("Gem Land Vidana"), under whom were villages in Ratnapura district the sole duty of whose inhabitants was to collect gems. "The Emperor (*i.e.*, Sinhalese King) used to fix the number and quality of gems they had to procure, and these he would present to his relatives and friends on the coast of India. In the same fashion they continued to procure gems on His Majesty's (the King of Portugal's) account . . . and so long as His Majesty was Lord of Ceilao there was not wanting Portuguese anxious to be Vidana Das Agras, although the position was not considered one of much authority among the people. It, however, involved the handling of stones of value, which they embezzled; nor did they lack accomplices and friends, for the King's Treasury is like an owl which all the birds pluck a feather from, and this is an evil that cannot be remedied."

Throughout the whole history of the island, from the time when Varthema, in 1505, described the beds of rubies which he saw in Ceylon, the precious stone has been a stumbling-block in the path of virtuous officials, not even excluding the Portuguese generals themselves. Outside Ratnapura, on the Colombo road, is a place called "The Moor's Field." A Moor who had collected a number of gems of great value in a box buried it here, and every night he used to come to look at his treasure by himself, until at last he went mad and could not find it. In his frenzy he raved about his loss, so that every-one in the neighbourhood was only too willing to help him to find the missing stones. All that field has been turned over many times, but no find was ever reported. It is said that in olden times one or two places were known where there existed a gem matrix—that is to say, the

THE TREASURE HUNTER

mineral formation from which gems originate—but in preserving the secret from the Portuguese it became lost altogether. Since then its rediscovery is a continually recurring problem. Sir. J. Emerson-Tennent mentions that Dr. Gygax found certain strata in which he said, "I firmly believe the rubies of Ceylon are originally found, and that those in the white and blue clay at Ballangodde and Ratnapoora are but secondary deposits," washed down by streams and floods.

The streams of Ratnapura are reputed to contain so many crystals in their courses that the water gains therefrom the clear pellucid character for which it is famous, and which renders it eminently suitable for the manufacture of mineral waters. It is said that on this account a lemonade in Ratnapura tastes as good as a whisky-and-soda elsewhere, but no exceptional increase in the consumption of the former beverage is noticeable. Perhaps owing to this fortunate attribute of the water Ratnapura abounds in Scotsmen to such an extent that the following anecdote is told of a young civilian who, being appointed to that station on his arrival in the island, applied himself to the study of the language. When asked, after a short time, by his Government Agent if he knew enough yet to speak to the people, he replied, wishing to display his quickly acquired knowledge of the local idiom: "Och! Ay! A ken it weel."

Below the old British fort which overlooks Ratnapura green flows the Kalu Ganga ("Black River"), where, in sheltered bays, the populace still pursue one of the amusements of the world that does not alter with the ages—namely, mixed bathing. Roman ladies and gentlemen bathed together; indeed during the later period of the Empire they made the rather revealing costumes of the Lido seem quite conventional by giving up the use of bathing dresses altogether, not only in the water, but also while sunning themselves later. In view of this interesting historical fact it is not surprising to discover that the Portuguese were accustomed to an occasional jaunt up-river, where no doubt the ladies displayed their dresses and ability to dispense with those hindering garments as picturesquely as the "happy group of up-river girls" who smile every summer so bewitchingly at Press photographers.

Portuguese ladies were by no means slow, while, if there were none available, their dashing countrymen were notoriously adroit in gaining the affections of the fair sex in any country to which their ambition led them; so the old Kalu Ganga must have seen many a lively evening party set out from the numerous forts and pleasure resorts that stood upon its banks.

At Dewal Kanda, not far from Kalutara, on a hill overlooking the river, are the remains of an extensive garden which belonged, so tradition says, to an ancient prince, whose residence, on the crest of the eminence, was no doubt appropriated later by one of the dashing captains of Kalutara.

When floating down-stream on a heavy-laden *padda* boat, with the moonlight turning each ripple and leaf to silver, it is not difficult to picture the Senhor, clad in doublet and flaring cloak, descending a winding path to the river with slow and stately step amid a crowd of respectful retainers, the fairest rose of Kalutara (probably not his wife) gallantly escorted upon his arm.

On reaching the water's edge the lovers board a boat, differing in no way from the modern craft, except that instead of the usual thatched roof it contains a curtained enclosure amidships for the reception of the hidalgo and his fair one, who, sustained by a jar of wine, and attended only by handmaidens, find the hours fly all too quickly as the unseen boatmen steer through a moonlit fairyland to the disillusioning dawn.

The Kalu Ganga, having been for centuries a highway of civilization, discloses at every turn of its course new instances of its influence upon the history or commercial enterprise of Ceylon. To leap in a paragraph from love to plumbago, although perhaps requiring an athletic mentality, is, therefore, not inconsistent with the rapidly varying considerations that rise to the mind as each bend of the river displays a fresh panorama.

After negotiating a stretch of rapids, some thirty miles from the mouth of the stream, a descending boat comes to Dumbara, where there is a plumbago mine, of which illustrations appeared in the Wembley Exhibition. Originally its shafts were sunk high up on a hill, from the heart of which the plumbago was obtained. This arrangement necessitated constant pumping of water from the mine by engines, for which expensive fuel had to be transported up the hill at a high cost. The superintendent of the mine removed this difficulty by tunnelling in from the bottom of the hill, arriving at his workings by rising galleries from below, and draining the water from the mine along the tunnel. Power was also derived from the stream to generate electricity, thus abolishing at once the drainage problem and all expenditure upon fuel. The mine is illuminated by electric light up to the working faces, and the plumbago is taken by rail from the foot of the rising galleries to the sorting sheds near the entrance. In boring from seam to seam compressed-air drills are used by the miners, whose stalwart forms, naked except for a spancloth, make an impressive picture, crouched in the dim light, amid a thick haze of dust, at the end of long narrow tunnels far from the earth's surface. In ascending to the upper workings a steep slope of rock, down which water rushes, has to be negotiated by the aid of a hand-rope—an exercise in which interest is heightened by the presence at the foot of the slope of a dark cavern, where the water dashes down a precipitous descent of some hundred feet to the main gallery.

There are two theories as to the origin of plumbago : the first, that water when very hot, due to volcanic influence, filtered into the rock seams or fissures, and, after cooling, left a deposit, which crystallized into plumbago ; the second, that the same phenomenon occurred, but that the medium was gas, not water. The plumbago lies in rock seams from an inch to two feet in thickness, whence it is chipped or hooked out with a long chisel. After being brought to the surface the larger stone and rubble is sorted out by hand from the substantial plumbago, then the remainder is treated by various processes, including sizing, winnowing, grinding, and rolling down inclined gauze trays, off which the little heavy lumps of stone roll, but to which the light, flaky plumbago adheres. After grading according to size and quality the plumbago is ready for sale.

The villages in this neighbourhood are full of small plumbago pits and sorting-sheds, where the trade is carried on in a much more primitive manner than in the mine just described. The mineral is so plentiful in the district that almost all the Gansabhawa paths glisten with minute particles dropped from the sacks of prepared metal that are carried down for shipment on the Kalu Ganga.

The continuity of existence of a great river

seems to influence even those who live upon its banks, enabling them to attain exceptional age. Urupelew Gamarallage Balahamy, for instance, must have been born about the time of the Kandyan War—in 1815—and although he could not remember that event he distinctly recalled the big Ratnapura earthquake in 1823. This venerable old gentleman came at last to view the world through eyes of indifference, as if he, endorsing the sentiments of Tennyson's brook, had become himself an embodiment of the everlasting spirit of Kalu Ganga.

It is from the lips of such veterans that, in the cool of the evenings, the old, old stories can be heard. Squatting with wrinkled arms on knees, and watery eyes fixed on a waving tree-top, while the toothless gums roll a "chew of betel" from side to side, the shaky voice mumbles placidly on, prompted occasionally by a grand-daughter who has heard the tale before. A story which illustrates well the Sinhalese sense of drama and humour is.

"THE RICE-POUNDER"

Brempy Singho and his wife Podi Nona had been married for more than a year, but still no child came to complete their happiness—an accident that was not only singular, but rather humiliating. Daily they took offerings to the temple, until what appeared to the would-be parents as a misfortune came to be regarded by the priesthood as a blessing. Finding that ordinary almsgiving was ineffective, although his finances were already reduced by the standard of devotion that he had maintained, Brempy, to his wife's horror, began to invite priests to the house with great frequency. On arrival the ascetics were asked to say a prayer, invoking the aid of heaven upon the efforts of their host to obtain an heir, then, at the orders of Brempy, Podi Nona, who excelled in the culinary art, had to provide a "*dana*," or propitiatory meal of delicacies such as would tempt the appetite of even the most abstemious Thero.

The meal finished, a further prayer with the same object was repeated, after which the holy man departed, well pleased with Brempy's devotional abilities. Podi Nona, who saw the garden daily depleted, and the *chena* crop dwindling beneath the heavy drain of such reckless hospitality, did not share the satisfaction of her guests. She realized that, however worthy the object, the liberality of the attempt to attain it must be checked; but, since her husband would hear of no decrease in the scale of his pious efforts, it was difficult to find a means to stop his extravagance.

One morning Brempy brought home a young priest fresh from a long fast, spread a white cloth on a chair for him to be seated, and asked Podi Nona to prepare a *dana*. "Wife," said he, "the Hamuduruwo is exceptionally devout, and also, still fasting, his prayers will be effective

BALAHAMY

I am sure. Hasten, therefore, to get the food ready, that after the strain of his meditations and starvation mine may be the merit to be acquired by supplying to him the wherewithal to break his fast."

"I have rice," replied Podi Nona, "but no vegetables. Run now to the *chena* and bring pumpkins and yams, that I may make dishes fit for the Hamuduruwo's ascetic palate."

Brempy hurried off, but Podi Nona, instead of starting to boil the rice, squatted near the priest, who, as befitted his calling, continued to gaze out of the door in meditation, or possibly in anticipation. After a little preliminary heaving and swaying, Podi Nona, with her face in her hands, began to cry and sob. She was handsome and very young, so that the comforting of her soul in its trouble was not outside the scope of ecclesiastical duties; in fact it would have been uncharitable not to take compassion upon her. When her sobs had subsided the priest asked: "Why did you cry?" "Because," replied she, after some hesitation, "my husband, whose habits I well know, will come back drunk, having stopped at the tavern on his way. He will take the big *kitul* rice-pounder from the corner there, and having killed you with it, as he has killed fifteen other priests, for whom he laid the same trap, he will bury you secretly. It is his form of madness, and I dare not let it be known, or he will curse me and I shall die."

The priest looked at the big rice-pounder;

it was unusually big; then, after peering carefully down the path to the *chena* where Brempy had gone, walked away rapidly in the opposite direction with as much dignity as he could command.

Before he was out of sight Brempy returned, shouting: "Why has the Hamuduruwo gone?" Podi Nona replied: "Because I would not give him the big rice-pounder; he took it up and admired it, but when he asked for it to be given to him as an alms-offering I refused. So he was very cross, and left, saying it was getting late." "Fool of a woman!" cried Brempy, "why did you not give it? What hope of a child have we now? I will take it after him; it may not yet be too late to appease him." Snatching up the rice-pounder, Brempy ran after the priest, waving it above his head and shouting, "Hamuduruwo, I beseech you to stop," while his wife watched from the doorway, trembling with excitement. As Podi Nona hoped, the priest looked round in alarm, to see his worst fears realized: the madman was chasing him, armed with the huge rice-pounder that had struck down so many of his luckless brothers in the faith. It was no time for dignity, unless he was to make the sixteenth priest in the maniac's bag. Away went the sunshade and fan as the reverend gentleman lifted up his yellow robes and ran his fastest, followed by Brempy, still shouting and waving his awe-inspiring weapon. The priest, untired by early morning work or a climb to the *chena* in the heat of the sun, outstripped his pursuer, and arrived in an exhausted state at the Pansala, where he told the story of his narrow escape from a madman whose hobby was enticing priests to his house on a pretext of offering a *dana*, in order to slay them.

Brempy never managed to persuade another priest to come to his house, however generous the *dana* he offered; in fact it was noticeable that the holy sect always avoided his society. But he never discovered why this was so, and it was not likely that his wife would tell him. It did not matter, because soon afterwards she presented him with a son.

As the quavering voice of the story-teller ceases he rises stiffly to go to bed; another night, if he still lives, he will speak again. But who can say? Anyway, an old man such as he will not be missed. Now he is tired; not like when he was young; then he would have sat up all night talking, and have gone to work too next morning quite fresh. He could have shown these school-taught boys how men lived in those days: nothing did he fear, not even devils, and there are plenty of those along the river bank.

In order to appreciate the old man's boast it should be explained that the jungles of Ceylon are infested with devils; numbers of people can be met who will describe in detail manifestations actually seen by them. In all editions the main characteristic is the unwinking glare of the blazing eyes, often associated with smoke or flame issuing from the mouth and a sulphurous smell, although it is possible that occasionally the actual smell in the locality is that of *arrack*. There can be no doubt that many firmly believe that they have seen these evil spirits ; so great is their conviction and so lucid their description that the listener, unless he preserves a profound scepticism, will begin to feel, like Felix, " almost persuaded " to belief. Spirits and evil influences may be ridiculed by advancing civilization, but in an atmosphere where they flourish it will be a very hardened unbeliever who, seeing at times a strange thing, will never feel a qualm of nervous doubt. When a person has come under the influence of an evil spirit the services of devil dancers are required to dispossess the devil of his victim, by means of a performance known as "Thovile." In the ordinary village household the necessity for this ceremony is an ever-present possibility, since at any time of day or night a devil will seize upon a person who happens to stray within the radius of his power. The importance of devils as a factor of village life is difficult for those who have not experienced it to realize, but the story of an instance of malign possession may show, to some extent, the reality of the phenomenon.

In the verandah of a small thatched house by the roadside sat two women and a boy, amid an array of cooking pots and utensils, which indicated that a meal was imminent.

"Punchi Banda—where is he?" inquired Podihami in vexed tones. "It is not often that he is late for his morning meal; more often it is he who, with unnecessary abuse, repeating 'Is it ready? Is it ready?' sits idle when he might be working."

"Since the tavern is closed, perhaps it may be a woman with whom he is talking," suggested Baby Nona, Podihami's ancient mother-in-law, who, having a sharp tongue and little liking for her son's wife, was a galling presence in the household.

"Is it not said," retorted Podihami, "that it is from their parents that children inherit bad habits?"

Silence fell. The meal—two curries and abundant rice—simmered invitingly, for Punchi Banda, in spite of his wife's derogatory remarks, was a good husband, earning a fair livelihood.

Podihami's impatience grew. "Arnolis," she said, "go now to Kokkumbura, beyond the rubber of Joronis Baas, where your father is working; tell him that the food is ready and come."

Arnolis rose unwillingly; the sun was hot and the food inviting—what hardship for a boy to endure! He disappeared in sullen displeasure.

Within ten minutes he was back, panting and pale with fright. "Father—he is in Joronis Baas' rubber; he neither speaks nor moves. He is dead."

Proclaiming, with many loud "*Aiyos*" and

hysterical moans, that some enemy must have assaulted her husband, Podihami, accompanied by a small crowd, arrived at the scene of the tragedy. The *arachchi*, a well-meaning soul, with less intelligence than importance, cautiously examined the prostrate man and found him insensible but not dead. It did not appear to be a case of assault, since there were no marks of external injury. What then could have caused such a sudden collapse? The solution of the question was not far to seek: a devil had struck him down on his way home. Was it not known that many devils haunted the village, especially the lonely rubber groves?

A melancholy little procession wended its way back to the house by the roadside, carrying the unfortunate Punchi Banda. A *vederala*, who was soon brought upon the scene, pronounced that the patient was in a high fever—not a difficult diagnosis, since he was now raving in delirium. In addition to the physician's potent concoctions a charmer was called, who exercised his powers to the full; but in spite of all efforts the sufferer showed very little improvement.

"How often have I not said," remarked Baby Nona sententiously, "that when one goes out one may or may not return." The astrologer, to whom admission was gained after a long wait, was pessimistic: Punchi Banda was under a bad star, and he might or might not recover; but the *vederala* stoutly affirmed that his medicines would bring about a recovery. "However," said he, "at present my prescriptions are unable to do their work, because I perceive that without doubt the devil that struck him down also entered into him, and there prevents the success of all my ministrations."

There was clearly only one course to pursue: a devil-dancing must be held, so that the devil who now malignantly possessed Punchi Banda should be persuaded or frightened into leaving him, then the *vederala's* medicines would be effective.

On the evening arranged for the ceremony the patient, who was just able to sit up, although still utterly dazed, was placed in a shed specially constructed at the side of his front yard. Before him was hung a white cloth, screening him from view for the present. Along the front of the shed was a row of small tables made of crossed bamboos, each bearing an offering to the sufferer's unwelcome tenant. Tied to one of the tables was a plump fowl, intended for the same purpose, although its ultimate fate lay in the dancers' curry. Across the little yard was a large square structure of bamboo, containing numerous openwork compartments, and crowned with graceful areca plumes. This edifice represented a city for the devil's reception, into which it was hoped that he would be enticed to enter. The four corner squares were known as the "*vidi*" (streets) of the city. On the side of the yard facing the house, with its back upon the road, was a small altar made of bamboo and plantain bark, upon which rested more offerings. The entrance from the road to the small dancing arena thus enclosed was beside this little shrine.

At about seven in the evening the troupe of dancers, comprised of a "*guru*" (teacher), his principal pupil, two juniors and a pair of tom-tom beaters, began their ceremony with a song and dance. Towards nine o'clock the performance, of which the whole trend was to persuade the devil to leave Punchi Banda, became more energetic; fresh offerings of areca flowers and betel were given, the tables were removed from the front of the patient's shed, and the cloth screen taken down so that he and his possessor might see the ceremonies. By now a large crowd had gathered, filling the verandah of the house and pressing into the arena entrance. Beside Punchi Banda sat his wife and his mother, the remainder of the family, with a few influential guests, occupying the shed. The dancers, one after another, wearing crowns, striped banyans and red waistcloths, took the floor, with the inimitable swagger of their kind, eyes directed upon the ground, feet wide apart, hips swaying and arms gesticulating in a circular downward motion, while the bells on their shins jingled rhythmically as they stamped their feet in time with the beat of the tom-toms.

As the hour of two in the morning approached there was a lull in the proceedings, while the dancers retired into the house to dress for the performances which would terrify the devil from his sanctuary in Punchi Banda, who sat gazing apathetically upon the scene. Suddenly, amid a wild outburst of tom-toming, a terrible figure rushed on to the dancing floor. At first it appeared to be a dancing tree, until the topmost foliage parted to reveal the coal-black face of a fearsome demon. With staring eyes and gnashing teeth it gibbered and nodded, alternately closing the branches before its gruesome features, and opening them again for a frightful display of demoniacal lunacy. The scene was eerie enough to frighten away any devil. The flickering, flaring torchlights, with their acrid smoke, increased the atmosphere of reality induced by the late hour and the preceding displays, while the trance-like pallor of the sufferer, as he gazed unwinkingly upon the scene, contributed to the general belief in the diagnosis of his condition.

"*Guru,*" groaned the apparition, "I like not this noise; I am hungry for food, see my teeth gnashing," and with a sepulchral clatter the huge fangs rattled upon each other.

"It is not hunger that chatters thy teeth, it is fear, O fiend," replied the *guru*, eliciting from the demon a blood-curdling groan and a frantic dance of whirling leaves and grinning jaws, until after further patter he fled, worsted by the noise of tom-toming and the shrewd wit of the *guru*.

Followed a crocodile, holding a torch in each paw and another lighted at each end in its mouth, revolving and contorting itself until it sank in a quivering trance near the door of the "city." Then a dumb devil, whose hopeless efforts at speaking were almost more horrible than the frenzies of its predecessors; next a deaf devil, and after him a dyspeptic, whose ashen countenance was sullen despair incarnate, and whose stomach pains were excruciating. Lastly, the hobbling spirit of rheumatism followed the others into the "city."

At this stage a sudden stir in the shed drew the attention of all. The patient had sunk back in a violent shivering fit; he was unconscious, and from his throat came nauseating, gurgling sounds, as if he had epilepsy.

"Behold," said Baby Nona, "it is the devil leaving him! To-morrow he may be well."

After a time the rigor wore off, and Punchi Banda lay quiet. At dawn the dancers left, well pleased with their night's work; but Punchi Banda still lay, whether in a trance or asleep it was impossible to say.

"Achchi," said Podihami, one hand on the patient's forehead, "the fever has left him."

"Fool," replied the old lady, "speak not fulsome words at this time or evil will befall. Who knows whether he will live or will not live?"

At noon Punchi Banda sat up, cursed his weakness, and inquired how long he had had fever. Of the dancing he knew nothing. He was cured. Whether due to his own strong constitution alone, or by virtue of the devil-dancing, who shall say?

CHAPTER EIGHT

ADAM'S PEAK

" Ape Budun : Api Wandinda.
Saman Dewindu Pin Labanda.
Sadhu ! Sadhu ! Sadhu ! Saaaadhu ! "

THE approach of the year's third full moon turns the thoughts of all good Buddhists and Hindus towards the Peak Pilgrimage. Although at this season the weather will probably be fine and warm, the journey by one of the longer routes is not a matter to be lightly contemplated; the primary stages by road and rail are rendered easier of late by special 'buses and cheap train tickets, but the actual climb remains no less steep.

All day long the pilgrims' haunting hymn, with its loudly vociferated chorus of "*Sadhu*! *Sadhu*!" throbs in the air, as the bands of devotees trudge stoutly through Ratnapura. Ahead of his flock marches the "*gurunanse*" (the leader of the gang), book in hand, chanting texts from the *Tun Sarana*, and frequently bursting forth into the familiar paean of praise, "Our Buddha! Our Buddha!" to which his followers reply, "Let us worship him!" The pilgrim company is usually comprised of members of the same family: first, a cluster of young men and women, in their best clothes, with umbrellas and numerous miscellaneous packages in their hands and on their heads; next, a poor relation or two carrying slightly heavier loads; then an elderly man with a lantern, straggling wearily behind, while the most youthful member of the party enlivens the toilsome path of his aged grandmother, who brings up the rear with many a shrill-voiced complaint and sarcastic sally.

"*Aiyo putha!* You may get as far as the Sacred Footprint, or you may not, as Heaven wills, but if this pace is to be kept up it is certain that you will return grandmotherless."

Then in a penetrating cackle, with a shrewd hit at the leader's profession: "I-hee, Gurunanse, because the son is a 'bus-driver, must the old mother also go fast?"

According to Buddhist tenets, Buddha, after a visit to Kelaniya, "rose, the Master, and left the traces of his footstep plain to sight on Samanakuta," as he journeyed through the air back to his Indian home. But the Hindu religion contends that when the god Siva came to Ceylon, to congratulate the war-god Skanda upon concluding the war between Suras and Asuras, mortals and immortals, he left his footmark upon the mountain as he passed on his return journey to heaven. In contravention of both these stories the Mohammedan version is that when Adam was thrown out of the Garden of Eden he fell here, leaving his footmark where he landed, to spend many years of exile on the mountain before he was permitted to rejoin Eve near Mecca. However, the *Voiage and Travaile of Sir John Maundevile, Kt., which treateth of the way to Hieusalem and of Marvayles of Inde, with other Ilands and Countryes*, relates that both Adam and Eve fell upon Adam's Peak: "In that yle is a great Mountayne.... And thei of the Contree seyn, that Adam and Eve wepten upon that Mount and 100 Zeer, whan thei weren dryven out of Paradys." When the Koran was written it is probable that the locality of Adam's penance was unknown, but the stories brought home by Arab sailors in the Eastern trade, of a marvellous footprint on the summit of a huge mountain in Serendib, crystallized the "Indian Mountain" of the holy record as "Al-rahoun," the name by which the Peak was known to the Arabs, because from a port of call in Ruhuna it could be seen towering high into the clouds.

The Chinese traveller Fa Hian ascribed the footmark to Foë, and the agrostics laid the responsibility on Ieu; but the Portuguese, not to be outdone, held that St. Thomas made it, and failing him the Eunuch of Candace, Queen of Ethiopia, who once paid a visit to the island. This diversity of tradition strengthens a theory put forward by Sir J. Emerson-Tennent that the universal sanctity of the "footmark" is due to the concentration upon one spot of the awe, veneration and worship commanded by a majestic, cloud-wrapped mountain.

The Peak itself is the home of the god Saman, who, for this reason, is regarded as the natural guardian of the Footprint, and is worshipped at a shrine on the summit. It is on account of this god's identification with the spirit of the sacred mountain that the thousands of yellow and brown butterflies who annually fly in clouds towards Buddha's Footprint are known as "Samanalayo." Entomologists aver that these little pilgrims are going to breed in a locality where there is suitable food for their caterpillars, but this materialistic doctrine deserves no credit against the well-known fact that they are going to worship at the Sri Pada.

There are three routes up Adam's Peak: from Kuruwita, twenty-one miles long, but steep only for the last nine miles; from Ratnapura, through Gilimale, which entails sixteen miles of steep ascents and descents; and the last and easiest, from Hatton, a stiff climb of only four miles. The enhanced merit acquired by going the difficult Gilimale way attracts to this route great numbers of pilgrims, for whom *ambalams* (resting-places) have been erected all along the road, and whose health is supervised by an inspector.

The ascent by this path begins at a village, of which the name means Vegetable-rice-stream ("Pallebatdola"), so called because here a very poor man, who could not afford to bring more than a few inferior vegetables with him on his pilgrimage, but nevertheless faced starvation in order to see the Footprint, opened the cloth containing his little store, to find the miserable stalks converted into substantial rice as a reward for his faith. The path lies through the thick forest of the Peak wilderness, where elephants are extremely common; in the dry season they are not often seen, but during the rains the few inhabitants of the neighbourhood, who live largely on platforms in trees, frequently keep a pot of water boiling, so that if an elephant tries to shake them out, or pull down the tree, they can pour the scalding liquid on to the tip of his trunk, and never again be bothered by the same animal. Up a steep rock on the path, where King Nissanka is said to have buried a store of treasure, there are ancient steps, of which the origin is variously attributed to several Sinhalese kings, according to the fancy of the historian. No one can tell the exact number of these steps, since no two pilgrims ever seem to be able to arrive at the same total when they try to count them. It has also proved to be beyond the power of elephants to uproot the iron handrail posts, which are cemented into the solid rock; although all are twisted into contorted shapes by the efforts of these animals to pull them out of their sockets.

Before many miles have been traversed the

younger pilgrims are taken to the edge of a deep ravine and told to call "Leniakka," when, a few seconds later, from the depths comes an answer, "*Innawa*" ("Here I am"). It was at this place that, while two girls, Leniamma and Leniakka, were collecting sticks, Leniamma missed her sister and wandered about calling for her, till, when she came to the brink of the precipice, the full force of the tragic circumstances dawned upon her, as from its inaccessible abyss she heard the faint answer of the unfortunate Leniakka, whose spirit still calls from the chasm into which she fell.

From Kuruwita the way is rather monotonous for the first ten miles, except when, after sudden heavy rain, the streams are in flood, necessitating a precarious crossing thigh-deep in a raging tide, over stepping-stones, for which the traveller must feel with one foot while balanced on the other in the swirling water. Where the ascent becomes steeper a glorious waterfall comes into view, crashing down a sloping face of rock, up which the pilgrim climbs, close to the hurtling torrent. During the day the heat, while clambering upwards in the dense jungle, is intense, making welcome resting-places of the frequent streams, where face and arms can be bathed in water flowing cool from the heights. It is noticeable that the keepers of the numerous wayside *boutiques* have exercised great circumspection in the choice of sites for their little stalls. As the weary climber turns a corner, after a particularly steep ascent, he at first despairs to see above him another two hundred yards of precipitous path, then, to his joy, perceives within a few more steps an inviting bench in the shade, and a hospitable host, anxious to sell him tea and cakes. The temptation to rest and refresh the exhausted energies is invariably too strong to be resisted, so that the *boutique*-keeper grows rich upon his knowledge of human frailty.

Since the pilgrimage is usually undertaken during the full moon, or Poya season, the pilgrims travel a great part of the way by night, with torches and lamps to assist them through the darker passages. In the *Life of Sir David Wedderburn* an ascent of the Peak by night is described: "We marched when the moon was supposed to have risen somewhere about mid-night. It was a strange scene, the glare of the torches falling on the bright dresses of the pilgrims as they climbed slowly up the pathway, which winds through jungle so thick as to meet close overhead. The effect produced in the uncertain light is that of a steep staircase tunnelled through a dense thicket of branches and leaves, as it might be the 'Hill of Difficulty' in *Pilgrim's Progress*."

At Haramitipana, three miles below the summit, the two routes from Kuruwita and Ratnapura meet. Here, where a small village of shops annually springs up around the large *ambalams* provided for the pilgrims by the charity of wealthy Buddhists, the travellers can rest comfortably before starting upon the last league which winds upwards to the Sacred Footprint at an alarmingly steep gradient. In the afternoon, when the air is clear of mist, the pilgrim can take his first uninterrupted view of the goal of his efforts. The huge pinnacle of rock, crowned with its tiny temple, stands out above the jungle-clad range of hills, clear to the last detail, with an awe-inspiring majesty that brings many to their knees in immediate adoration. The remaining three miles, known as the "Air-League," is largely composed of steps, to whose numbers more are added yearly by enterprising and pious worshippers; but in the cool of the night the devotee scarcely notices the difficulties of the way, so elated is he by the nearness of the Footprint and the clarity of the mountain air. Now more than ever he shouts "*Sadhu*! *Sadhu*!" as he tops each ascent, while as the summit grows closer the *gurunanse* and his flock alternately recite and repeat a text for each step they climb. At the foot of the final pinnacle, which towers above the crest of the range, is a large *ambalam*, where the pilgrims gather to shelter from the bitter cold wind, preparatory to climbing the ladders that lead to the shrine through the waning moonlight.

These ladders are of very ancient design, made of iron, with wide flat rungs, far apart, and the breadth of two modern ladders between the uprights. They lie on the surface of the rock, at an easy slope, up which the ascent is assisted by equally antique chains hung alongside from iron pins driven deep into the earth. These chains, with curved links almost a foot long, are of so unique a pattern as to render possible the legend that they are the same as were seen by Ibn Batuta, a Moor, who ascended the Peak in 1347, when he found, "at the foot of the last pinnacle . . . a minaret named after Alexander the Great; steps hewn out of the rock, and iron pins, to which chains are attached, to assist the pilgrims in their ascent." Similar chains on the Hatton side are described by Sir Vivien Majendie, who climbed up from there on 1st January, 1896: "In the height of the pilgrim season (which begins in January) the scene is most extraordinary, men, women, old and young, some almost decrepit, some who actually die on the way . . . and many who have to be pulled or carried up, people from India, from China, from Japan, from Burma, from Spain, from Siam, from Ceylon, from Africa, priests and laymen, princes and paupers, may be seen striving, toiling, perspiring upwards. . . . And on the way, particularly at Oosamalle, the Buddhist pilgrims suspend long threads of cotton from the trees, for here, tradition has it, Buddha stopped to repair a rent in his robe. Then presently the pilgrims reach, as the ascent becomes steeper and more difficult the curious ancient chains which have been affixed there for centuries to assist those who would ascend. It is even alleged that these chains were affixed by Alexander the Great, who journeyed to Ceylon in 330 B.C. Anyhow, we know they are extremely ancient, if not quite as old as this, for Marco Polo mentioned them in the thirteenth century. The pilgrims call these chains 'The Chain of the Creed,' and on each link they wearily utter some word or expression of devotion."

This stream of humanity which works its way up from Hatton, without acquiring so much merit as those who come by the longer routes, contains the majority of the Hindu pilgrims, Indian Tamils from the up-country tea estates; stout Mohammedan traders, whose figures prohibit the more arduous paths; and European visitors, frequently including ladies among their numbers.

The summit of the Peak is a small plateau of some two hundred square yards in extent, enclosed by a stone wall, built close to the edge of the surrounding precipice, while in the centre of this compound, and occupying about half of its area, rises the rock, approximately ten feet high, bearing the Sacred Footprint, over which is built an open hall supported on pillars.

Rajanna, a minister of King Parakrama Bahu (1164-1197), was the benefactor who erected the first edifices at the summit, for the convenience of pilgrims and the better preservation of the relic. "He caused the great forest to be hewn down and a public path made; and then he went to Samantakuta and worshipped the Footprint there, and set up an image of the god on the ground within the courtyard of the shrine and built an open hall over the foot. He also caused a wall to be built round it; and as he was a man of great forethought he fastened the open hall with great chains to posts of iron, and so made it firm." There is no image "within the courtyard" now, except a small figure of the god Saman, and the "great chains" holding down the roof have given place to cement beds for the feet of the pillars. An illustration in Tennent's *Ceylon* shows them, but whether drawn on the spot or reconstructed from ancient descriptions is not disclosed. Between the wall and the edge of the cliff is a well of clear water, from which the pilgrims drink, not only to quench their thirst but also to gain benefit from the element springing forth in so holy a place.

A few buildings have stood for many years at a lower level than the summit, upon ledges on the eastern side of the pinnacle, but in 1926 a new large *ambalam,* made of corrugated iron, was constructed against the wall of the temple compound on the west, with its stone foundation laid on an artificially cut shelf. The situation looks precarious, but the brilliant red colour of the building evidently inspires confidence, since a pilgrim was observed, some five miles down the mountain, gazing fervently upwards and murmuring ecstatically in a kind of chant: "*Sadhu*! *Sadhu*! *Tagrum*! *Tagrum*! *Ratu teinta*!" ("Alleluia! Corrugated iron! Red paint!".)

The Footprint, as detailed by Lieutenant de Butts, in 1841, "is slightly, but indelibly, indented on the smooth (horizontal) surface of the rock, and measures nearly five and a half feet in length by thirty inches in average breadth." The outline has now become rather faint, and, unless cleaned of the debris of oil and vermillion powder placed upon it by pilgrims, is almost indistinguishable. The resemblance is more conventional than realistic, especially as regards the toes, but this style of delineation renders it by no means less venerable. The small open temple that covers the relic is extended in a portico over a platform on the rock, where pilgrims stand to worship, separated by a stout railing from the Footprint, which lies to the western side of the hall, with its toes towards the observer, surrounded by a ridge of cement about three inches high, to prevent water from draining into the depression.

It is said that the present Footprint is a replica of the original, which, impressed upon a gem of incalculable value, was covered by the god Saman with the rock that forms the point of the Peak, as a precaution against theft. If the extinction of the temptation can be so called, it was a most effective precaution.

The offerings are collected by a trustee, and

their value credited to the account of the Buddhist Temporalities' Committee, a lay body which administers the proceeds in the furthering of Buddhist doctrine.

On coming to the wall which encloses the summit an experienced Buddhist *gurunanse* waits in the entrance gap to collect his flock, before shepherding them all in, one close behind the other, with a united chorus of praise. As they press through the opening, palms reverently joined aloft, and heads bowed forward, many fall upon their knees in a silent ecstasy of prayer, while women sob and laugh hysterically, crying "*Sadhu*! *Sadhu*!" without cessation, though so emotionally stirred and worn with fatigue that they are completely unconscious of their actions. When the first glamour of arrival has abated the pilgrim band collects around its leader, who distributes the individual offerings which each is to give; then, with deep obeisances, all climb the few steps that lead to the Footprint. Gazing at last upon the goal of their long pilgrimage, they kneel in prayer, before pressing forward to place upon its rocky surface the offerings, of cloths, money and silver ornaments which they have carried so far. Standing at the rails that guard the sacred object from harm, they burn oil that has been brought solidified inside coconut shells, and lay areca flowers before the holy emblem; then, descending from the rock, they kneel again in the little compound, reciting texts and prayers.

As they crouch, droning a monotonous chant, in the deep shadow of the rock cast by the moon, the awe inspired by an age-old worship compels whole-hearted reverence. Far below, the encompassing hills of dense forest lie bathed in a silver haze, from which arises faintly the song of toiling pilgrims. Black against the moon are silhouetted figures in all attitudes of worship, continuously ascending and descending the time-worn steps that lead up the mass of rock to the Holy Imprint, beneath its slender outlined tracery of roof, where, within the flickering radius of an oil lamp, rapt faces appear and reappear, as they lean forward to put the treasured offering upon the Master's Footprint.

The wind is deadly in its biting cold, the smell of stale burnt oil standing in puddles is intolerable, and the refuse of foot-soiled, rotting, floral offerings contaminates the air, but in the chill hour before the dawn an all-pervading sense of sanctity obliterates every other impression with an irresistible dominance.

Hindu pilgrims begin their operations by perambulating round and round the enclosure jingling small bells and repeatedly shouting: "*H'ro! H'ra! Govinda!*" Elderly estate coolies, who at every step for the last two or three hours have ejaculated "*H'ro! H'ra!*" become so wound up that they cannot stop saying it, and can be heard slowing down by degrees under the ministrations of their daughters, until the continual repetition gradually declines into a spasmodic monotone, finally dying away in a few faint "*H'ras,*" to a dazed silence. After pealing a big bell, which hangs in a corner of the compound, one ring for each ascent that has been accomplished, a practice common to all religions, they retire, and squat in small parties around "Amma," usually a forceful matron of decided character, who apportions out the votive articles that they have brought.

This procedure entails considerable argument, Periasamy protesting with voluble irrelevance that it was he who was to give the two-rupee note, while Sollamuttu, being known to be young and also foolish, was to have given a fifty-cent piece. However, "Amma" squashes dissension with vituperative ease, and peace is restored before they start on their round of devotion, prostrating themselves in spotless white cloths upon the muddy rock, amid the pools of oil and water. The Hindus pay more active attention than others to Saman Deviyo, who resides in a small shrine, with a broken piece of glass before his face, at the foot of the rock, where, in a tray standing on a tripod, large quantities of oil are burnt. The flame of this oil can be seen from great distances, as it leaps and flares above the mass of broken bottles and coconut-shell containers that are smashed and thrown with their contents into the tray.

Huddling around the fire for warmth, the pilgrims constantly rake and turn the flaming shards, while, amid profuse advice from all his relations, Perumal scrapes together a little pile of soot, which is carefully folded in a scrap of newspaper, to be carried home as a sure preventive of all ills.

When dawn draws near a sense of excitement pervades the waiting throng, who, packed tightly within the enclosing walls, and mounted on the rock itself, all face intently towards the east, in order to welcome the sun as he, too, rises to worship the Sacred Footprint. The first lemon-tinted lighting of the sky, behind the conical peak of Totupola, draws a murmur of anticipation from the watchers, as the vast range of the Kandyan mountains springs forth, dense black from the misty grey of the waning moonlight. Two huge rays shoot across the sky, and the hills show up against a blood-red background, in which the clouds assume fantastic shapes: here a house; there a child with her hair in a "*konde*" (knot); and to the north, with its hand stretched forth towards the yet-hidden sun, a gigantic figure, whose contours are slowly changing. The hair grows long about the shoulders, the nose is flat, the mouth prominent, the stomach large, and there can at last be no doubt, it has a handsome tail. Suddenly recognition steals upon a Tamil labourer; there is an excited whisper, then a voice breaks forth: "See, it is Hanuman who points to the coming sun." A student in the crowd laughs, as befits one superior to such superstitions, but his unjustified scepticism, more assumed than real, is ill received by all who know that the signs of the sky are never meaningless. The light brightens, turning to blue above the red, after passing through a delicate shade of green. The two rays are nearly joined above the hills; in a moment the sun will appear; a woman cries tremulously, "It comes," and is curtly told to shut up; then a clear black line shows round a tiny semicircle of molten gold, above the crest of the range, and the shout goes up from the worshipping multitude: "*Sadhu*! *Sadhu*! *Govinda*! *Govinda*!" Ever so slightly the sun's lip rises before—once, twice, as far as ten times—it flickers deliberately up and down, eliciting an ecstatic cry: "See, the sun-god bows to the Sacred Footprint. Let us worship."

As the golden disc ascends, the bottoms of the valleys change from grey to blue, while details show up one by one with a sudden distinctness that recalls the turning on of electric light. Meanwhile all press round to the western side of the enclosure, where lying in a perfect cone across land and sea, with its point a hand's-breadth up into the sky, stretches the shadow of the Peak, one of the unique sights of the world. The mounting sun illuminates in the foreground a level white sea of rising mist, pierced with bright green islands that are the tops of hills, while beyond lies the level plain of the Western Province. But where the Peak interposes, the valleys are still discernible, as was the whole landscape before sunrise, in a murky gloom, which terminates in the clouds with the square silhouette of the wall that surrounds the Footprint. Outside the dense body of the shadow, but all converging upon the sky-borne point, are lighter bands of shade, caused by rays that have just caught the edge of the obstructing mountain sufficiently to diminish without obscuring their light.

Although the intrinsic beauty of the scene is incomparable, the overwhelming hugeness of this titanic shadow concentrates the attention to the exclusion of more aesthetic considerations. The Hon. Ralph Abercromby, F.M.S., writing about the shadow in *The Philosophical Magazine* for January 1887, summed up his explanation as follows: "There are not many mountains that are over 7000 ft. (Adam's Peak is 7352 ft.) that rise in an isolated, well-defined pyramid. Still fewer can there be where a steady wind (the North-East Monsoon) blows up a valley for months together, so as to carry the morning mist to a suitable height and distance on the western side to catch the shadow of the Peak at sunrise."

The first Englishman to ascend the Peak was Lieutenant Malcolm, of the 1st Ceylon Regiment, who reached the summit on 27th April 1827, although various European travellers, including Marco Polo, had adventured so far in olden times.

Once the ladders upon the final pinnacle are

passed, the descent, though trying to the knees, is not arduous. Uplifted by the thought of an object accomplished, and merit gained, the pilgrims go down with light hearts, acclaiming the upward toilers whom they meet with cries of, "*Karunavai*," a propitious expression, meaning "kindness." As each landmark is reached, the memory of the fatigue of the ascent returns with a pleasurable glow, reflected in the good-humoured faces of the returning travellers. Then, like Chaucer's Canterbury pilgrims, the elders recount "tales told by their parents," of the times of the Sinhalese kings, when Raja Sinha waged deadly war against the Portuguese, and Guards of the Kandyan kingdom fought battles with the Hollanders on the frontiers of the hill country. "When I was a boy," says old Arnolis Appuhamy, "three men went to look for a cave that is hidden in the wilderness not far from here. Having found it, if a man looks inside, he will first see much writing on the rock-wall, then beyond, in a second small room, he sees the object which he most on earth desires. It may be that he did not know before that the thing, or person, he sees is the fulfilment of his longings, but at the cave he will have no doubt. For different people it will be different things, but no one seeing the bait has ever resisted the temptation to go in and secure it. Once a man has gone in he never comes back. I think a devil eats him; at least that is what Silinduhamy said happened to Weerasinha, without whom he returned from the wilderness. This jungle is full of strange things, but if you keep to the path you are protected from all evil while on the pilgrimage to Sri Pada. Mind, though, Punchi Nona, if you stray but a few yards from the track you may be seized by a demon. It has happened. I speak the truth, who am an old man, without cause to lie."

So at last, footsore, but content, the weary company reach the main road, where the waiting 'buses hoot and roar, ready to carry them home to all parts of Ceylon. The noise is tremendous, small boys yelling the destination of each vehicle in violent competition, while touts, seizing upon unwary passengers, endeavour to persuade them that the 'buses they represent are the only safe conveyances in which to travel, even though they may not be bound for the destination that the harassed fare desires. At last all are in; with a final shriek of "*Panadure*! *Panadure*! *Panadure*!" fierce clashing of gears, roaring of engines, tooting of horns and stentorian back-fires, the lumbering motor careers through the fleeing populace, at a speed far beyond the safety limit, on its adventurous journey. "*Aiyo*," murmurs grandmother, "now have I endured the great difficulties of the long pilgrimage, to die in an accident to the "bus-eka.' "

CHAPTER NINE

JAFFNA

IN very ancient times there lived a blind minstrel, in Southern India, who was terribly worried by a nagging wife. At last, being unable to bear her railing longer, he announced his intention of going to Lanka, a project which she ridiculed with a pert allusion to his prospects of becoming the owner of large estates and many elephants. On arrival at Anuradhapura the minstrel asked to interview the Tamil king, but was not allowed to do so, for fear that evil might befall the Royal House after seeing so ill-omened an object as a blind man.

Besides his musical talents, the minstrel had most unusual powers of perception, which were of infinite service to him when he realized, although he was not told, that the king was in the same room as himself, behind a curtain, dressed as an archer. Comprehending that a test of the powers of which he had proclaimed himself the possessor was in progress, he ingeniously sang an extemporary *sloka*, comparing the king with Rama, the mighty bowman and hero of Ceylon, accompanying himself on a "*yal*" (lyre). Presumably in order to clear up any subsequent suggestion that the minstrel's apt song was a coincidence, the king put on his queen's robes. Immediately the minstrel sang another ode, which indicated clearly enough that he knew of the change, although the wording might be considered in these days a little indiscreet. Lastly, the king put on his own robes, and was greeted at once by a contemporary version of *God Save the King*.

The king, recognizing talent, rewarded the minstrel handsomely by presenting him with some tusked elephants, and the northern part of his domain, called Manattidal (the sand-heap), which was not then very valuable, for reasons disclosed in its name.

The minstrel sent a letter to India, not only announcing his success, and rubbing it in to his wife, but also inviting settlers for his kingdom—an invitation that was accepted in such force that he was soon king of a large community, who, by their unfailing industry, turned the sand-heap into a prosperous land and called it Yalpanamnadu (The Land of the Lyre-Minstrel), the name by which it is still known in Tamil, although the Dutch shortened it to Jaffna.

The subjects of the minstrel, who were fishers, were the ancestors of the present Karia people or fishermen. It might be considered that this convincing story would fill every requirement in accounting for the Tamil name of Jaffna, but hard-headed historians have put forward a theory that the first settlers in Jaffna were a section of the Panar people of Southern India whose tribal distinction was a facility for playing on the *yal*.

Jaffna was first known as Naga Dipa, or Naga Island, from the large number of Nagas who lived there, mingled with Yakkhas, who spoke a language called Painachchi. In this tongue one Kanabhuthi wrote *The Seven Stories*, of seven hundred thousand *slokas*, each *sloka* of some length, and one hundred thousand *slokas* for each story; a best-seller, perhaps, in its day, but now rather overshadowed by the shorter modern type of book. These people, too, came from South India, and, during their time, the name again changed to Manipallavam (The Sprout of Ceylon); later, when ruled by the Chera kings, it was called Cherendib, or Serendib, the island filled with precious stones upon which Sinbad the Sailor was wrecked.

In the third and fourth centuries B.C. the Sinhalese occupied the Peninsula, where they left their traces, in the shape of place-names and architectural remains. Dr. Pieris, working upon information gleaned from ancient documents, made extensive excavations at different places, finding at Kanter-rodai a *vihare* and stone Buddha together with innumerable Sinhalese relics, which were placed in a museum at the Jaffna Police Court. The site of the *vihare* is a mine of archaeological remains; half-an-hour's work with a *mamootie* will unearth beads, coins, pieces of broken bangles and sculptured stones, while the ground is littered with the cut-stone ruins of ancient buildings. The Chunnakam Buddha and *vihare,* also found by Dr. Pieris, are of even more archaeological fame than those of Kanter-rodai, as the Buddha is intact, and was removed to the Residency garden, where it stands beneath a tree, near that which sheltered the Vallipuram Buddha, who was given to the King of Siam.

Following the Sinhalese period came the time of great Tamil power under Elara, 206 B.C., and his successors, who took the centre of Tamil activity south to Anuradhapura and Polonnaruwa, whence, having reached the zenith of its prowess, it retired, as the centuries passed, to the Peninsula.

The last great dynasty of Tamil kings of Jaffna began, it is said, in the twelfth century A.D., when the Southern Indian Chola Empire fell, and many of the nobility, with their retainers, migrated from the chaos to North Ceylon.

These kings of Jaffna rejoiced in the title of Ariyachakkaravarthi, and one of the first of them, who had been educated in Madras, after building a great palace at Nallur, founded the Kandasamy Temple, whose yearly festival is one of the wonders of the East. There are still extant a few traces of their early influence, the most obvious being the "*Nali*" (poll-tax), introduced by the first king. The south-west wind, which blows with great violence in Jaffna from June until September, is known in Tamil as "*Solakam*" (the Cholas wind), because, to traders from Ceylon along the Indian east coast, it was the wind which blew from over the Chola country. There is also a Tamil lullaby, evidently Chola in its origin, which refers to the baby it is intended to soothe as an Indian Prince: "Oh, my Baby Princeling, thou hailest from Nellore in the North Country."

The Chola emigrants, who set sail from the Pennai river near Madras, came during the night hours into the Jaffna lagoon, and anchored there. In the morning their ladies, waking up and finding themselves again apparently in a river such as they had left, cried, looking no doubt reproachfully at their respective husbands: "Why, we're back in the Pennai river again!" The husbands were so pleased at having scored off their wives that they called the place Pennai, in commemoration of the event, and Pannai-thurai it remains to this day.

The Tamil kings continued to use the Nallur Palace, built on the site now called Sankily Tope, as their headquarters, while outside the fortifications grew the ancient town of Yalpanam. At Copai there was a fortress, of which the only remaining wall is now included in a house. As the power of the Jaffna kings increased, so did their splendour. Near the Nallur Palace, and at Copai, large finds of coins have proved beyond doubt that they had their own coinage, stamped with the figures of the king and a bull. Unfortunately, nothing of their palace remains except a tank, which, like a moat, is built round three sides of a central pavilion, whence steps lead down to the water at a shallow place for bathing. The tank is known as the "*Yamanari*," a name said to have been acquired when a king, who had been on a pilgrimage to India, threw into it some of the sacred waters of the Yamana, or Jumna, which he had brought back with him for that purpose.

Again possibly it is called after the Yavana or Arab Mohammedans, now known as "Moors," who first settled in that locality, and who were driven thence by an ingenious device. The Tamils killed some pigs and threw them into the Moorish wells, so that the Mohammedans, when they came to draw water, found it all turned into pork soup; they, therefore, shifted their quarters to the eastern end of Jaffna, where they still reside. This story bears a likeness, in theory at least, to Lamb's essay on the origin of roast pork.

In 1560, during the reign of Sankily, a king whose conduct was as unscrupulous as it was barbarous, Constantino de Bragança, Portuguese Viceroy of India, outraged by Sankily's piracy, decided to conquer Jaffna. On 22nd October, 1560, twelve hundred Portuguese disembarked at Pannaithurai and presently began to march on Nallur.

The description of the battle given by the Rev. Father Gnana Prakasar, in his book, *The*

Kings of Jaffna, reads like a passage from Prescott's *Conquest of Mexico* :

" They were headed by a Priest bearing the Banner of Christ, and formed into five divisions, the Viceroy bringing up the rear. The Prince (Sankily's son), who was distinguished by his chank shield, offered a stout resistance at a narrow passage, but was repulsed with some loss. The next day the invaders continued their advance in the same order. Their way lay through jungle and they had to push back the defenders from wall and stockade. When they arrived within sight of Nallur they once more encountered the Tamils, drawn up in two lines before the wall, which was made of stone and clay with strong bastions, mounted with artillery and some entrenchments occupied by matchlock men. The first line resisted bravely, but it was pushed back with heavy loss on the second, which was protected by the fire from the bastions.

" This, however, was not effective enough for the enemy (Portuguese), who gained the wall with a great dash, and, making a breach in it, poured into the wide street of the city leading to the fortified Palace of the King within. The three pieces of artillery which the Tamils had hidden under palmyra leaves, and fired as they entered, did little harm to the enemy—only eight were killed—who rushed in with greater determination, carrying the guns and driving back the Tamils, with much loss.

"The Viceroy, whose charger had been shot under him, fought his way to the vanguard on foot amid a cloud of arrows and bullets. Here the Prince had appeared, assisted by a force of Moors and Badagas, who, under the effects of bhang, fought with reckless fury, while from the adjacent gardens and house-tops arrows were poured on the invaders without cessation . . . At last the Prince was forced to retire. . . . The invaders were now masters of the City, which the soldiers began to plunder. Among the prisoners were the Prince's wife, who afterwards became a Christian, and other ladies of rank.

"As night had drawn in, the Viceroy pulled down some houses and encamped for the night in front of the parade-ground facing the Palace, intending to storm it on the morrow. But, during the night, Sankily slipped away with all his treasures, after setting fire to the Palace, directing the Prince to follow him to the fortress at Copai, with the Queen and other women . . . Bragança hastily arranged for the occupation of the city and made for Copai, only to find that the King had abandoned that fortress, leaving at its entrance the heads of twelve of his chiefs, whom he had probably beheaded for advising him to make peace with the Portuguese."

Bragança sent four hundred men in pursuit of Sankily towards the south, but he escaped, drawing his pursuers after him, farther and farther from their headquarters, until, on the southern side of Elephant Pass, he turned upon them ; but again the Portuguese were too strong for the Tamils, and Sankily sued for peace. He was allowed to resume the government, and so had opportunity to plan an insurrection, which was successful for the time in driving the Portuguese out of Jaffna.

In October, 1591, they came back, under André Furtado de Mendonca, landed at Columbutturai, and swept all before them, but, even then, constant risings continued, until, in 1624, General Oliveira checked further trouble with a heavy hand, banishing the last king to Goa, where he was beheaded, and razing the great Nallur Temple to the ground. The last princes of Jaffna bequeathed their sovereignty of the kingdom of Jaffna to the King of Portugal in 1623. Whether there was any undue influence exercised in connection with this bequest is a moot point.

The Portuguese then settled down peaceably in Jaffna, establishing their government offices, whose entrance gate alone remains in token of past glories, on the site of the old Nallur Palace. The first Portuguese place of worship in Jaffna was near the present Roman Catholic Cathedral, and was called the "Chapel of the Cross," because miraculous crosses appeared there, but later it was moved to Nallur and rechristened "Our Lady of Victory," to commemorate the conquest of Jaffna in 1591. When numbers of

Portuguese traders settled around Pannaithurai, the church was brought near to them, and rebuilt in 1614 close to the site of the present Dutch church in the fort. The Moors were driven off to the present Moor street, leaving the neighbourhood entirely for the Portuguese residents, whence it received its yet existing name Parangithurai.

In 1624, General Oliveira built the fort, in the same place as the Dutch fort now stands, round the church, which was then called "Our Lady of Miracles"; later still it seems to have been dedicated to St. Francis. The Portuguese built churches in various parts of the Peninsula, but the only one not yet entirely ruined, or repaired out of recognition, is at Changanai, where the walls are yet standing and the chancel is intact, with a unique vaulted stone roof. The pillars of the nave and the west end were pulled down some time ago, as being unsafe. At Vaddukoddai, Pandaterruppu and other places are churches now in use, in the hands of the missions, but these buildings have been restored and repaired by the Dutch and their subsequent owners until very few of their Portuguese characteristics remain.

Although little of their architecture exists, the Portuguese have left many descendants, comprising a large community known still as Portuguese or "Mechanics." They are all artisans—bootmakers, watchmakers, and men of kindred trades—and have been attracted largely, in modern times, to motor engineering works. The present generation are forgetting their mother tongue, but the older people all speak a semi-Latin medley which they term Portuguese. The Dutch classified the Portuguese of mixed descent, for military purposes, as Toepasses, who had a Portuguese father and a Ceylonese or Indian mother, and as Mestises, whose parentage was *vice versa*.

Upon the Tamils, especially in Roman Catholic communities, the impress of Portuguese rule is still evident; among their names are found Avurampillai and Matalanapillai, the equivalents of Abraham and Magdalene, together with numerous other adaptations, while the fisherwomen all wear the little short jacket introduced in the Portuguese period. At the threshing-floor many cultivators draw a cross over the paddy heap to indicate, outwardly at least, their devotion to the Faith that was forced upon them, while among the older generation, both Hindus and Christians, the turban is commonly tied in the form of a cross, and on almost all bulls the brand mark includes the same sign. For a like reason, on Hindu fasting days, when people eat off plantain leaves, they put the leaves among the palmyrah *olas* of the roof when the meal is over, for fear that the Portuguese, who forbade the practice of fasting as idolatrous, should find the leaves and punish the offenders.

In 1658 the shadow of the Dutch fell on Jaffna,

when the great Ryclof van Goens, having taken Colombo, marched northward, took Mannar with ease, and arrived at Chavakachcheri. Then the Portuguese paid for a joke they had played on the "*mudaliyar*" (chief headman) of Tenmarachchi. This *mudaliyar* had asked for a white wife, and, ever polite, the Portuguese replied that it would give them great pleasure to send him one. In due course, amid great rejoicing and vast preparations for her reception, the bridal palanquin arrived, but was found to contain a pure white bitch, with a gold collar. To pay off this grudge the *mudaliyar* sent word to Jaffna that the Dutch were sailing up the lagoon, then, while the Portuguese were preparing to resist a landing at Jaffna, he led the Dutch army by land, unopposed, up to the outskirts of the city. Such are the penalties of bad taste.

After some fighting, the Portuguese, under Joas de Melo de Sempeio, fell back into the fort. accompanied by many Tamil refugees, in all some five thousand people, for whom there was neither adequate accommodation nor food, except rice which was already bad. All the refugees were lodged in the church and its cloisters. Owing to the strength of the fort, which van Goens himself said "deserved the name of fortress more than any he had seen in the whole of India," the siege lasted three months, in spite of the order in the Dutch army that "every one of the race of swine (Portuguese) found armed should be put to the sword."

So closely were they hemmed in that no supplies could be obtained, the bad rice set up an epidemic, while the water was contaminated by unburied corpses, so that at last hunger and disease proved too strong, and on 2nd June, 1658, the Portuguese surrendered, on terms which were not quite fairly carried out by the Dutch. Two thousand one hundred and seventy had died, and the three thousand odd survivors, who took three days to stagger out, were not treated in the manner that their gallant defence deserved.

Ribeiro, in his account of the surrender, says: "We were stripped naked, both men and women, and searched by the Fiscal in a most degrading manner, all our things being taken and guarded in the House of the Governor. We had much to thank them for this carefulness, for they guarded them so well that none of us ever saw a single thing again in his life."

The men who did not take service under the Dutch were sent to Batavia, and imprisoned there, but the ladies were kept in Jaffna.

At a meeting of the Army Council on 28th June, 1658, Ryclof van Goens ordered a day's celebration of the great victory, in terms that indicate the sedate satisfaction of the Dutch leaders at the capitulation of the fort: "Whereas the General and Admiral of this Armada, and his Extraordinary Council, having considered the great mercy . . . which Almighty God has so graciously shown us on this expedition, having not only by His heavenly aid conquered for our superiors the whole island of Ceylon, but also purged it of popery and abolished and expelled its idolatrous practices . . . it seemeth good . . . to appoint the 10th of this month (that will be a Wednesday) as a special day of thanksgiving."

(FACSIMILE OF SIGNATURE OF RYCLOF VAN GOENS TAKEN FROM THE GOVERNMENT ARCHIVES)

The Rev. Baldaeus, needless to say, preached a thanksgiving sermon, on a very appropriate text, Exodus xvii. 15, where, after Joshua had discomfited Amalek and his people with the edge of the sword, "Moses built an altar, and called the name of it Jehovah-nissi."

The fort was then sacked, but was in too filthy a condition to be occupied for some time; later it was rebuilt at leisure as it now stands, the main work being finished in 1680 and the outworks in 1792. Except that a road has been built between the wall and the lagoon, the Dutch architecture is unchanged, and in perfect repair, thanks to the fact that it has never had to withstand siege or attack. The Dutch garrison consisted of 287 Europeans, 56 Mestises, and 17 Toepasses—in all, 360 men; not a very large force for a pentagonal fort enclosing about four acres, with a large bastion at each corner of the ramparts.

The main fort wall is 50 feet high and 40 feet wide at the top, separated by a picturesque moat from a most elaborate system of sunken outworks, whose parapet at ground-level forms the crest of an extensive glacis, now used as an esplanade.

Within the fort are the Dutch church and King's House, the residence of the Dutch Governor. The church, both inside and out, is a perfect example of the architecture and ecclesiastical furniture of the period. It contains two huge pulpits, choir stalls, governor's seat and organ loft; all on an immense and massive scale, while the walls and floor display numerous memorial tablets to departed burghers of distinction. Among these notabilities lies a Dutch lady who, with gentle cynicism, scoffs at the friends she has left behind. Her epitaph reads "*Fui, quodes, sum, quoderis*" (I was what you are, I am what you will be). One of the bells, now in the vestry, bears the inscription: "*N.S.*" (Nossa Senhora) "*Dos Milagres de Jaffna Patao*" (Our Lady of Miracles of Jaffna)—identifying it as a relic of the original Portuguese church that stood in the western corner of the fort. The other bell is in St. Michael's Church, Polwatta, Colombo.

King's House is palatial, in size at least; all the rooms, of vast dimensions, are in line, fronted by a lofty verandah, 70 yards long, with thirty-two pillars, so that a long walk is entailed from the main bedroom at one end to breakfast in the dining-room, at the other. It is a pleasantly enough situated residence, but not one that could be advertised as "neat and compact and containing every modern convenience." Sinnatamby, its faithful guardian till his death, was an institution, almost of historical interest; his career as a servant of Government, or at least of Government servants, dated back to the early days of Sir William Twynam, while he himself was a privileged character, whose conversation, intelligible after some experience, was a delightful medley of scholarly English, in which the word "otherwise" appeared with surprising frequency, both appropriately and inappropriately.

The old cannon, which are left in their embrasures, are all stamped with the Dutch

="*Vereenigde Oost-Indische Campagnie*" (the United East India Company), while above the V.O.C. on some is an A, signifying that they came from Amsterdam, and on others a Z, showing that they came from Zeeland. There are five or six guns made on lines less ornamental, but apparently more serviceable than the others, judging from the absence of corrosion; these bear the foundry mark, "CARRON, 1789," and were evidently made at Carron, in Scotland, the oldest ironworks in the British Isles, as armament for the army in the East. A small English brass cannon is now at the Police Station, with the mark of the British East India Company thus:

On the south-west bastion is a large belfry where the garrison bell was rung, both for time-keeping and for raising the alarm if necessary. In Jaffna Fort the English barn-owl can be found; several birds inhabit the murky fastnesses of the roof of King's House and nest in the blocked drainage outlets of the ramparts.

The Dutch, by means of forced labour, dug a deep channel—still in use for shipping—the whole length of the Jaffna lagoon, although how the coral rock was cut below a man's depth in water, without machinery, remains unexplained.

Dutch churches are found in every part of the Peninsula, some in use, others in ruins, but all of them testifying to the energy of the Rev. Baldaeus and his colleagues.

In Jaffna main street are many old Dutch houses, with unsuspected walled gardens and compounds behind them, whose peaceful seclusion and old-world atmosphere render it easy to catch visions of the homely Dutchman, dozing away the hot hours with his pipe and glass of gin.

Robert Percival, Esq., of His Majesty's 19th Regiment of Foot, wrote in 1803: "A Ceylonese Dutchman . . . rises early, about six, and either goes to walk or sits down by his door in a loose robe and nightcap to smoke a pipe. This with a glass of gin, which is called a *soupkie*, fills up the interval to seven. A dish of coffee is then handed him by his slaves, and his lounging posture and tobacco pipe are resumed for another while. He then gets up, dresses, and goes to business, or more frequently to pay visits—a mode of spending time of which his countrymen are particularly fond. In these visits the Dutchmen usually take a pipe and a glass at every house to which they go. If they have leisure to prolong their visit they take off part of their dress and put on a little nightcap, which they bring with them on purpose, and then set themselves to smoke and talk till noon. Their dinner-hour is about twelve.

"At Mynheer Conrade's, at Colombo, I found the dishes extremely well dressed, and the fish, in particular, appeared exceedingly palatable to an Englishman. After dinner they resume their favourite regale of smoking in an undress and then go to sleep for an hour. As soon as they are again dressed they either go abroad to pay visits or receive company at home; and this, with another pipe, fills up the interval till supper is announced at nine."

It is a matter for comment, adverse or favourable, according to inclination, that "the conversation of women, which has tended so much to humanize the world, forms very little of a Ceylonese Dutchman's entertainment."

Mr. Percival seems to have been impressed by this phenomenon almost as much as he was by the discovery that "the Dutch ladies had a custom of cracking their joints, and rubbing them over with oil, which rendered them uncommonly supple."

Outside the fort the Dutch general had a second residence, now the house of the headmaster of Vembadi school, whence a legendary subterranean passage runs, under the moat, to King's House in the fort. Material proof of the existence of this tunnel was thought to have been discovered when a workman, who was effecting repairs to the headmaster's house, found that the floor of a bedroom sounded hollow, and, with a sharp tap of a crow-bar, made a hole through into a vaulted chamber

A CEYLON DUTCHMAN IN A.D. 1800

beneath. There was every reason to think at first that this was part of the passage, but on examination it proved to be a small room, possibly a sentry-box, against the wall of the old house, above the original ground-level, which had been subsequently built over when making a more modern extension.

The coming of the British in 1796 begins an entirely new era in Jaffna, ending with the enterprising Tamil community of to-day, whose unique customs and fascinating characteristics form subject-matter for a separate chapter.

CHAPTER TEN

THE TAMILIANS

THE title of this chapter is selected not only for its resemblance to *The Virginians*, but because the Rev. Dr. Pope, whose correctness of language few will doubt, uses the name Tamilians repeatedly and advisedly in his *Tamil Handbook*. This book, the refuge of the student, is at the same time the despair of the industrious pupil; its length, despite the wise adage at the beginning, "Difficulties will vanish as you learn," is sufficient to appal even the most energetic, but the tedious pages of grammar are relieved here and there by flashes of the Doctor's humour, like milestones on the journey to knowledge.

Such a milestone is Lesson 35, an unparalleled example of the correct method of turning English into Tamil. The corresponding Tamilized English, which is printed below each word of the vernacular, renders the primary difficulty of translating the idiom of one language into that of the other easy to master, by its comic phraseology.

LESSON 35—A STORY

"(Every word in this tale is in use and every form deserves attention. Let the learner go over it often and carefully consult all the references.)

The Honey-Drop Tumult.

"A Muhammadan a great in town to the bazaar having gone, honey which will buy the time, a drop-honey below was split. Of it upon a fly having come it alighted. That fly, there-which-was a lizard having seized, took. That lizard the bazaar-man's cat having seized, took. That cat the Muhammadan's dog having bit it, put. That dog the bazaar-man having beaten, having killed, he put. That bazaar-man the Muhammadan having cut down, he put. That Muhammadan the other bazaar-men having cut down, they put. Those bazaar-men the Muhammadans having come, having surrounded, took. The Muhammadans them having surrounded having seen, for the bazaar-men many persons came together. And those, and these, hand having mingled, a row having made, in that side a hundred persons, in this side a hundred persons, to die indeed, the town all having feared, utter confusion having suffered, a hurried removal it took."

A certain Professor Schoff, whose enthusiasm for the study of Tamil is not perhaps shared to excess by the average learner, speaks of the above methods of expression in terms so glowing as to be almost extravagant, especially when applied to the story of the honey-drop tumult: "How peculiar and truly Tartaric this wonderful concatenation of sentences and intervening words! A sentence runs on in long periods like a majestic stream . . ." It is unnecessary to quote his words further; a glance at the final sentence of the honey-drop story shows what he means.

One of the most remarkable exponents of the Tamil speech, correct yet colloquial, was Percival Ackland Dyke, Esq., who was appointed a cadet on 15th May, 1822, and who died in Ceylon on 9th September, 1867. For many years he was Government Agent of Jaffna, in which capacity he earned the title of "Raja of the North," and the well-deserved credit for many of the beauties of the town. Along all the open roads are tulip-trees, planted under his direction and nurtured during the dry seasons, under his personal surveillance, by a host of gardeners, whose employment depended upon the success of their activities. In Nallur he planted what is probably the finest avenue of Mahogany-trees in the world, but his most valuable bequest was the Residency in the Old Park, a beautiful building, the walls of whose rooms are coated with the same sort of "*chunam*" (lime enamel) as covered the *dagobas* of Anuradhapura. Mr. Dyke is said to haunt the upper storey, but as this was not built in his time the ghost yarn appears to have no foundation.

The names of Dyke and Sir William Twynam, who followed him, a second raja, will live long in the history of Jaffna's prosperity. Sir William, dying in Jaffna at the age of ninety-six, left a museum to St. John's College, which comprises a complete collection of every conceivable object of interest in the Peninsula, especially including the different implements used by the castes in their hereditary industries.

These castes are the relic of Indian civilization, still forming the basis of Jaffna social life. The average farmer belongs to the Vellala caste, descended from the ministers of the kings of Jaffna; working in his house is to be found the Kovia or domestic-servant class; the Nallava and Palla men, who were soldiers and cultivators, specialize in tree-climbing to tap *toddy*, and, in a rather indifferent method of fishing. The dhobies, barbers, carpenters, goldsmiths, ironsmiths, oilmongers, musicians, weavers, dyers, garlandmakers, palanquin-bearers, and numbers of smaller communities, are all meticulously segregated, even living, to some extent, in their own separate villages; while the fishermen of varying types—Karias, Thimilars and Mukkuwars—are a class apart.

Brahmins are all priests, although many of the lesser temple officers come from the Pandaram or mendicant caste. By consent usually placed last, but by no means least useful, are the Pariahs. Every Vellala family has an hereditary coterie of retainers to fill all domestic spheres, recruited from each caste, according to its traditional employment. In the days of slavery these household officials performed their duties gratis, and were fed; now, in most cases, they claim their fees; but still the system of hereditary retinue continues as in feudal times. The occasional refusal of one of these ancestral dignitaries to function is a fruitful source of feuds. The subject of caste, though intensely interesting, is not one that lends itself to amplification, for fear, as would appear to be inevitable, of treading on someone's toes.

The village life of the people, in spite of small peculiarities essential to Jaffna, is in all its main features parallel to that of any other country, eastern or western. Marriage, or otherwise, births, funerals, church and temple festivals, petty quarrels over wells and land, constitute the daily interests, while, as in the West, the youths congregate at small bridges and culverts to smoke, swear, hatch mischief and tell doubtful stories, leaving the elders to sit in a conspicuous position near the market and utter profound maxims upon very trivial occasions.

Some of the Tamil proverbs are of peculiar virtue: "You cannot turn a lean into a fat ox in seven days" is frequently controverted in S.P.C.A. prosecutions for emaciation; "The surest-footed beast of all, the elephant, may slip and fall," meets the occasion of a rascally headman caught at last; "The distant bank, when it is seen by cows on this, appears more green," expresses human dissatisfaction; "If one sets out auspiciously one will return triumphantly," a warning against impetuousity; "Never start to do anything if the lizard chirps, it is fatal to success"; "However high a little bird may fly it will never become a hawk"; "If a crow bathes three times a day it won't become a stork"; "If your hoppers are ready, eat them"; "Like a leopard crying because a goat has got wet"; "Will a bottle gourd grow when a different seed is sown?"; "If a man is unfortunate, though he may find work, he will not get his hire," are proverbs with obvious morals; when a very unfavourable proposition is suggested there is a saying that it is "like asking a chicken if it wants to be made into a curry."

The all-pervading *cadjan* fences exercise a rather limiting effect on the mental as well as the physical horizon, leading to endless disputes; when a stick dies each of the owners of the land on opposite sides of the fence endeavours to be the first to replace it one or two inches within the other's land, thus, in the course of years, increasing the extent of his own land by a few square inches. This encroachment is strongly resented by the adjacent owner, who had intended to do the same himself, leading to a fight, or at least to mutual abuse by families—father against father, wife *versus* wife, and so on down the scale, till even the newest infant on each side of the fence hurls invective at its equally vehement opponent in arms.

Next they appear in the police court, where, if allowed to do so, every member of each family will file a separate plaint on various charges against each member of the other, followed by a land case of vast dimensions and tedious length in the civil court, continuing until both sides have spent all their money, when they subside into a condition of verbal hostility till death intervenes. It is not suggested that all the inhabitants of the Peninsula are constantly engaged in such pastimes—far from it; they are some of the most hard-working people on earth, but it is difficult to find a family in whose history a contest of this kind has not figured.

In the life of the Hindu population fasting is an important feature; at least once a week a day is spent without food; no doubt excellent for the digestion, but rendering the day's routine arduous and uncomfortable—so much so that frequently people are heard to say that as it is a fasting day it will be impossible to perform some ordinary duty. The beneficial effect upon the health, however, no doubt outweighs other considerations.

A wedding is a most complicated ceremony (this platitude does not apply exclusively to a

Jaffna wedding): an auspicious day must be selected to plant the first post of the "*pandal*" (festive arch) at the respective parties' houses, and to melt gold for the "*thali*" (marriage necklet). The family dhobies and barbers are assembled on the wedding day to bless the bridegroom and lay cloths, on which he walks to the bride's home, interrupted by blessings from the ladies of all the intervening houses with whom he is on speaking terms. On arrival at the bride's residence he is again received by women, and a younger brother of the bride washes his feet, when at last he sits under the marriage *pandal* with the lady of his father's choice.

A sacred fire burns before them and, while Sanskrit hymns are sung, the bride's parents offer the right hand of the bride—containing betel leaves and areca-nut as a sign of prosperity—to the bridegroom, who accepts it, standing, in both his hands, under the blessing of a priest; meantime the *thali* and "*kurai*" (bridal cloth) are handed round among the visitors to be blessed. The couple then exchange garlands and the *kurai* is put on, followed by the tying of the *thali* round the lady's neck by her husband, who is then offered milk and plantains by her. Each has a sip from the cup of milk, when the priest presents both with a little parched paddy, which they unitedly throw upon the sacred fire. After blessings and congratulations they retire to the bride's room, where she serves him with rice and curry, eating of it after him, followed by betel and areca-nut, when, having feasted with the assembled relatives and friends, the husband takes his wife home. The ceremonies are then complete. It is a fine point of etiquette for all relations to be invited to the wedding; exclusion is a direct and almost unforgivable insult, calculated to foment rancour in the family for generations.

Following up the career of the happy couple, it is noteworthy that a child should for the first time taste rice on an auspicious day. This ceremony takes place on the completion of the child's sixth month, and it is important that he should begin his alphabet on the first day of his fifth year, on the same day attending the temple for the first time in the capacity of a worshipper.

At this stage, for sentimental reasons, the couple can be left to live happily ever afterwards, while attention is turned to an unknown patient nearing his end, in whose case no personal interest has been aroused. He is surrounded by relations and friends, some of whom have come out of affection, others in a final effort to recover debts he owes them.

His eldest son attends to his wants, and, after life is extinct, closes his eyes and mouth, when a close relation goes into the front yard and, with hands to head, wails "*Aiyo!*" thrice. This is the signal for all the women relations and neighbours to gather and lament loudly, beating their breasts; if the *paterfamilias* has expired the form of lamentation is: "Our father is dead. *Aiyo*! Our father is dead"; at the same time it is not unusual to lie upon the ground, throwing dust upon the head.

After a funeral women frequently cannot speak except in a husky whisper for several days. The corpse is washed with three pots full of water, gingelly oil applied, and wrapped in a new cloth; then rice is put in its mouth and it is conveyed to the cremation ground. The leading officiant at the ceremony, in this case the eldest son, walks three times round the pyre, with a water-pot on his left shoulder and a torch or firebrand in his left hand; at each circuit the barber knocks a hole in the pot; then the pyre is lighted at the head end, the eldest son drops the water-pot behind him and walks away without looking back, followed a little later by the remaining relatives. Various ceremonies are performed at the funeral house for sixteen days, at the end of which period an effigy of the corpse is again burned and the funeral is over.

In the event of sickness so severethat medical skill fails it is common to resort to magic, even of a sinister kind. A sufferer from diabetes was told that a human sacrifice alone could save him, so his sister, being a midwife, took the opportunity, after her services were completed, of stealing the baby from a house where she had been employed and depositing it in a well. It is not a matter for despondency that the patient died within a short period.

The "*Pelli*" is a charm only to be prepared by advanced magicians, and composed of the most revolting ingredients, of such deadly power that it is firmly believed that if the correct "*manthirams*" (Sanskrit incantations) are said over it, at the right conjunction of planets, the person against whom its evil influence is directed will die within twenty-four hours.

The "*Chunium*," a milder but useful charm of numerous unsavoury components, including human bones, is used for good or evil purposes, according to prescription, by means of secret introduction into the house of its object, where it is left to work its beneficent or disastrous mission. Many a man (suffering from too much *arrack* and too little exercise) becomes easily convinced by a practising magician that an enemy has introduced a *chunium* into his house, which can be removed only by expensive and risky methods. In such a case. a magician undertook to remove an evil charm from his patient's house, having foretold that the identity of the sufferer's enemies would be revealed by the death of their cattle. On the day after the *chunium* was said to have been miraculously removed an enraged farmer took to the nearest police court an habitual criminal, alleging that he had caught him in the act of administering a dose of poison to a cow. The habitual admitted this, adding that the magician had given him ten rupees to do it.

A more attractive *chunium* is the love philtre, of which part of a "*sempakam*" (jungle crow) is an invaluable ingredient. The discouraged lover must, with the aid of one wise in such matters, introduce his *chunium* into the house of his beloved, if possible concealed under the floor. After she has stepped on or over the hidden charm nothing will restrain her from joyfully accepting her lover's proposals. Whether this form of *chunium* exercises a lasting effect would appear to be doubtful.

The concoction of "*kumbam*," another form of evil magic against the person, is regarded with such horror that it comes within the scope of law as criminal intimidation; in such a case a special magician was hired to pursue his cult, in the presence of the ill-wishers, at a deserted house, where the séance was discovered by a headman, who produced in court the book of words, including terrible incantations woven around the names of the victims. Fortunately, perhaps owing to the timely intervention of the law, the objects of the outrage lived.

No one should kill a snake on a Tuesday or a Friday (one should not do anything at all on a Thursday), but if a tic-polonga so escapes it will live to be two or three hundred years old, when, after developing wings, whose touch is deadly, it finally bursts, bringing forth a mixed bag of centipedes, scorpions and tarantulas. The sacred cobra, of light colour, the "*nalla pambu*" (good snake), although very venomous, is never killed, because, having learnt wisdom, it appears only on Fridays; but the big "pariah cobra," who eats eggs and chickens, can be slain almost at any time. The late Mr. J. P. Lewis was told at Kayts of the *Kodalai podian*, a snake which causes a person on whose back it falls to go bent double for the rest of his life, while at the Pearl Fishery at Marichchukaddi he saw the "*Irutalai manian*" (two-headed snake), "a very bad snake which can move in either direction, ahead or astern, and can drink at either end." There are evidently some advantages even in being a snake.

A number of beliefs and theories are extant about trees; the shade of the "*vembu*" (margosa) is extremely healthy, so also it is lucky to make door frames and windows out of its wood, whereas it is disastrous to build satin-wood into a house—a belief that certainly gains colour from actual modern instances. The baobab, it is said, was introduced by Arab traders as fodder for their camels; there is a big tree of this kind in Delft. The banian is the home of gods and devils, but the shade of the tamarind, though cooler than any other, is unwholesome; so much so that even in 1803 Robert Percival says: "It is a general order with the troops never to allow horses to be picketed in its shade."

Mr. J. P Lewis wrote of this tree: "Both Sinhalese and Tamils agree that the shade of a tamarind is cooler than that of any other tree. So pleasant is it that there is a saying in Jaffna that the son of a widow should not sleep under one, apparently because it will make him lazy and will, therefore, result in his failing to work for his mother. A characteristic of the tree is that, when there is a shower of rain, it penetrates very slowly through its small but densely crowded leaves to the ground below, and it is a long time before the leaves begin to drip. Hence the episode of the poet Tiruvallavar and the poetess Avaiyar. The poet fled for shelter from a shower of rain to a banian-tree, while the lady preferred a tamarind close by. The poetress hailed the poet in a couplet more forcible than flattering :

> " 'You fool of the empty leaves,
> Come under the little leaves !'

" Whether the poet gallantly took the advice (*verb. sap.*) or countered with another couplet was not told me."

The poetess Avaiyar has left to posterity traditions about herself that are, perhaps, more widely known than her poetry. Dr. Pope, who calls her (translating from the Tamil) " the wonderful old woman," relates that " she was one day sitting in the porch of a temple with her feet stretched straight out before her, not considered to be a very respectful position in the presence of a superior. The officiating priest rushed out to her with the question :

'Are you not ashamed to stretch out your feet in the presence of the Lord ?'

"'Very true, sir,' she replied; 'if you will show me where the Lord is not, I will go and stretch out my feet there.'"

Poetry, however, is not confined to celebrities. "Kamban, a great master of Tamil rhythm, passing by a well one evening heard a cultivator, as he watered his field, sing the line:

'On the leaf of the bamboo.'

Then the man, having completed his number of buckets of water, ceased at once his work and his song. Kamban was struck with the line and said to himself: 'What can be on the tiny leaf of the bamboo? Probably to-morrow morning the labourer will begin his work with the next line of the song.' Accordingly, with the dawn, he stood by the well and was rewarded by hearing the man, as he drew his first bucket of water, chant the second line:

'Sleeps the little drop of dew.'"

The learned Doctor, in concluding this note, remarks, in italics: "*Moral.*—There is plenty of poetry and sentiment in the Tamil people if you can only get at it."

As in Sinhalese districts, a special language is used at the threshing-floor, composed only of auspicious words, lest the demons, being displeased, should carry away corn from the grain heap ("*poli*") to the floors of others whose conduct has been more exemplary. No one with a basket or bag should be allowed to pass by the threshing-floor while the grain is being measured, or the demons will use them as a means of transport. A more material suspicion seems to actuate this custom.

After the measuring is over, the most important person present picks up a few grains with his mouth and spits them out, holding his right ear with his left hand and his left ear with his right hand; thus the grain is "defiled with saliva," rendering the demons powerless to move it.

When the corn is ready to be stored, two varieties of deities, Kanıyalar and Annamar, must be propitiated, the one with cooked rice, fruit and vegetables, the other with a roasted fowl and *arrack* and *toddy*—offerings which are later eaten by the *vellalas* and their Palla assistants respectively.

The measuring of the paddy into shares is frequently attended by disputes, more or less violent, resulting in the inevitable lawsuit; but litigation, fortunately, can often be curtailed by one party or the other taking an oath at a temple to decide the issue. The oath has a final and satisfactory result in almost all cases where it is taken, the losing party knowing, if the oath is true, that justice is done, and if it is false that all the village knows it to be so and will not allow the swearer to forget the fact. This practice is not confined to Hindus:

Roman Catholics also swear before the altar in their churches. There is a firm belief that evil results attend the taking of a false oath, especially at the small "Muniappa" temple outside the walls of Jaffna Fort, which has acquired a great reputation for supernatural power, owing to the circumstance that a District Court suitor, after swearing a false oath there, died suddenly the next day.

In Jaffna temples the gods most commonly worshipped are Ganesu or Pillayar, his brother, Kandasamy or Subramaniam, and Siva, their father. In Sivan temples are also found shrines to Pillayar and Kandasamy, his principal sons, with smaller niches for Vairavar and Aiyanar, although separate temples dedicated to them individually flourish throughout the Peninsula. Dhobies worship Aiyanar, while Pallas favour Annamar; Pariahs especially venerate the Nachimar, Virgins of the Vanni, seven of whom committed suicide rather than fall into the hands of their enemies; their eunuch guards, the Annamar, followed their example, and all have been deified. Hanuman, the monkey god, is the guardian of all Vishnu or Perumal temples, of which there are only four in the Peninsula. There is also a god called Anumar, whose devotees and devil dancers display peculiarly simian activities, both in their grotesque performances and, so it is said, in private life.

A detailed account of all the Hindu deities of

Jaffna would be a work of stupendous dimensions and purely theological interest; the gods mentioned are those who figure more largely than others in the numerous temples, and do not include uncommon cults. Each god has his "vehicle," or incarnate form, a representation of which is to be seen in the outer court of the temple, for use on festivals—Siva, a bull; Kandasamy, a peacock; Vishnu, a cobra.

The annual temple festivals usually last twenty-five days; on each day a separate ceremony is performed, culminating in the procession of the deity round the temple on the twenty-fourth day, and the "*thitum*" (bathing of the god at the sacred tank) on the twenty-fifth. At Nallur Kandasamy Temple and at Maviddappuram these festivals attract huge crowds of pilgrims from all over the Hindu world. New streets of shops, Indian and Jaffnese, are set up, and the neighbourhood is a dense mass of people, through which flows a stream of men and women performing vows, made while in some extremity of sickness or distress, to be fulfilled in case of relief. The commonest undertaking is to roll a given number of times round the temple, or even as far as six miles along the road from the home of the devotee, while, to increase the discomfort, men can be seen with spears and skewers stuck through their cheeks and tongue. Women do not roll, but drop on their knees and bow their heads to the ground every two or three yards. The rollers show surprising skill and speed, all avoiding puddles if possible, as the sun on a wet body produces sores and blisters when rolling, although it is extraordinary how little their skin is grazed.

The "Kavadi" procession, a popular form of devotion, not so strenuous as rolling, entails carrying over the head an ornamental arch, covered with brilliant cloth and having a column of peacock feathers at each corner. By way of improvement the carrier can stick skewers through his cheeks, or walk on sandals covered with spikes, points upwards; as an alternative he can be driven by means of a rope, attached to some two or three hundred hooks inserted in the skin of his back, stopping at intervals to perform an intricate dance, whose movements are indicated to him by sharp pulls on the rope from his driver. Cases of men cutting themselves with knives are not uncommon, and frenzied worshippers occasionally become possessed by a species of devil, which throws them to the ground, where they writhe and kick in amazing contortions, to the embarrassment of their immediate neighbours in the crowd, who are unable to avoid their gesticulations.

At the climax of the festival the deity is placed in the carved processional car, elaborately decorated for the occasion, and hauled round the temple "*vidi*" (procession path) by the worshippers, amid the dense crowd, who hand up offerings of fruit to the Brahman priests riding upon the car platform. Half of each offering is kept for the temple and the other half handed back to the donor with the blessing of the deity. It was at this time that, in the olden days, women cast themselves in frenzy beneath the moving wheels and were crushed to death.

Festivals constitute the relaxation of the worshipper as well as his religious exercise; it cannot be said that devotion is the sole object of the teeming thousands who attend the final days; the cheery holiday faces all show that at least they take their worship in a happy spirit, engendered on the way, jostling along the road amid thick clouds of dust, shouting, exchanging repartee, and racing in bullock-carts, to the imminent danger of pedestrians. The journey to the temple is the Jaffna replica of the road to Epsom on Derby Day, the same good will and excitement prevails among the throngs of travellers, every one of whom enjoys the trip with a fervour that only a traditional holiday can induce.

The less important ceremonies occur at night, especially in smaller temples, whose devotees are at work by day. Beneath Kitson lights the congregation—consisting as a rule only of men, who may wear nothing above the waist—gather in the outer hall, to watch the proceedings, after the fashion of a theatre audience, during the performance of *pooja* and purification

HINDU WORSHIPPERS HANDING UP OFFERINGS TO THE PRIESTS ON A PROCESSIONAL CAR

ceremonies within, where space does not permit of their entering.

In many temples, until the deity is ready to be carried out for worship, it is the duty of dancing girls to entertain both the waiting god and congregation with their art in the outer hall. Musicians, with lute and tom-tom, work up a brooding melody, when, to the chinking of bells on her ankles, the artiste, a pretty girl, attractively dressed in rich clothes and jewellery, enters the circle of light, broad hips swinging, feet jingling, and hands gesticulating in time to the now unrestrained music. After a preliminary exhibition of steps and adornments the girl executes an allegorical dance, embracing a topic such as the love story of a queen in Hindu history, an exemplification of an incident in a Tamil literary classic, or a *motif* characterizing, in the poetry of motion, the actions of a devotee, who, fascinated by the presence of the god, is compelled to remove her jewellery and lay it at the feet of the deity, in an ecstasy of generous abandon.

The scene is impressive to a degree—beneath the garish light, amid the silent, absorbed crowd, the girl pursues the graceful evolutions of her art, to the frenzied music of her accompanists, in an atmosphere pervaded by the aroma of sandalwood and jasmine, while within, through the open door, can be seen the reverent figures of those officiating in the *pooja*, around a fire, whose flames only serve to intensify the dark brown gloom of mystery beyond, in the sacred depths of the holy of holies.

A special sort of sea-shell—the right-spiralled or whorled chank—is used in temples for pouring sacred oil and water. Among the many millions of chanks with spirals running left-handedly, that are annually fished up by the Indian Moor divers for the purpose of sale to make lime, very occasionally a right-handed one is found, worth about Rs. 100 or Rs. 200 to its owner, when sold to a temple.

Very rarely, too, these valuable chanks are picked up from among the inevitable litter of shells around the shores of the lagoon. The chank-divers carry on their work on much the same lines as pearl-fishers, but, for obvious reasons, are not allowed to fish within the pearl areas. Different types of Jaffna fishermen have each their own exclusive methods. The Karias of Passayoor and Karayoor use a kraal net, in which the fish wander along a wall of netting until they find themselves in an enclosure from which there is no escape. In the inland lagoons *kaudis* are used, fences made of sticks stretching right across from shore to shore, with gaps every few yards, leading into traps. Inshore the hand-net is possible; the fisherman, stalking his prey, flings his net, which spreads out into a circular shape in the air, attached from the centre to his wrist by a line, and falls flat above the shoal of fish, when the weighted edges at once sink, so enclosing the catch.

The *vidu valai* is an ingenious contrivance which needs several men to manipulate. A rope about fifty yards long, with pieces of coconut *ola* tied to it every foot, is paid out, then, leaving a man at each end of the rope, the remaining fishermen get ahead with a large hand-net, which they spread and allow to sink, standing round it in the water, waist-deep, like people about to shake a carpet.

The two men with the rope then advance upon the net, dragging the rope, with its *ola* tags, along the surface of the water, in a big crescent behind them. All the fish near the surface rush in terror ahead of the rope into the outspread net, which, at the crucial moment, is lifted with the catch.

The "*kudu*" (fish trap), like a lobster-pot, is placed on the bottom in a circle or small bower of stones, at a depth of three or four feet ; after a day or two sediment and fronds of seaweed become attached to the trap, and the little unsuspecting fish, who come to play hide-and-seek among the stones, choose its dim, inviting recesses as a hiding-place, from which they never return.

The lagoon fisherman employs a canoe ("*vallum*") made in India, but the deep-sea fisher from the north coast uses a catamaran, made of four logs of wood, shaped and bound together, which he sails with amazing skill in all weathers.

Deep-sea fishing is done with a long net

stretched from one catamaran to another in a continuous advancing line, which catches all the fish that strike it, or by a single catamaran, from which a long floating wall of netting is laid, into which the fish, including huge turtles and dugong, swim and are entangled—the latter, known in Tamil as the sea-pig, is a great prize, worth up to sixty rupees in the fish-market, where the Moormen rush for it, as they say that, being denied the pig bred on earth, the pig that lives in the sea was specially created for them: when cut in slices it looks just like bacon.

Wells are of supreme importance in the Jaffna Peninsula, where rain, except from October to February, is very scarce, and rivers and streams are non-existent; it is, therefore, of peculiar interest that Jaffna wells are of a unique type.

Almost all are inexhaustible, but brackish if sunk very deep, and tidal in a greater or less degree, due to sea-water percolation through the coral stratum. This percolation is so slow, and varies to such an extent, according to the height of the tide, that the slight rise and fall of water in the wells does not correspond with that of the sea, except that, during the North-East Monsoon, all wells on the western side of the Peninsula are a little deeper, when due allowance for rainfall has been made, owing to the fact that the wind, driving the water in the Bay of Bengal in a south-westerly direction, raises the level of the Jaffna lagoon eighteen inches.

The Puttoor well has become famous because, although in the centre of the Peninsula, it displays tidal propensities in a marked degree, and for that reason has been subjected to various experiments. The total depth is about one hundred and fifty feet, the bottom hundred being salt water and the top fifty fresh, with its surface approximately at sea-level. The level of the water changes three times a day, wherein it differs from the sea; also the water in the well is usually found to be sinking when the tide is rising. In 1824 and 1897, when attempts were made to use this well for irrigation purposes, the pumping engines failed to alter the level of the water or to check its rise and fall, although the enterprise had to be abandoned, as in the dry season the water was too brackish.

It is said that the well claims three lives yearly, but this story is not borne out by facts, although, in view of its unusual characteristics, it is not surprising that supernatural powers are ascribed to it. It can be tested by experiment whether a stick thrown in at Puttoor sinks and comes out in the sea at Keerimalai; for fear of prejudicing the mind of anyone wishing to try it, the results of previous experiments will not be divulged.

Once upon a time an unfortunate Tamil man owed a vast sum of money to a *chetty*, on which interest at 40 per cent. was demanded. Unable to pay, he went to the *chetty* and prayed for mercy, declaring that unless he was absolved from his debt he would cast himself into Puttoor well. The *chetty* was adamant. The debtor, therefore, fixed a date and time at which, if not released from his burden, he would hurl himself into the pit.

As he expected, the *chetty* came to see whether he would carry out his intention, and, at the appointed moment, in the presence of the *chetty* alone, no word of absolution forthcoming, the debtor jumped into the well, causing even the hardened heart of the usurer a little uneasiness. As not a trace remained of the suicide, his moral murderer concluded that, like the sticks, he was on his way to Keerimalai, where he would be "found drowned."

The debtor, however, who could swim, had concealed himself, just above water-level, in one of the deep recesses, hollowed out by tidal action, that line the sides of the well. When the *chetty* was gone, having climbed out, he wrote a letter to an imaginary brother, describing his financial plight and his intention to commit suicide. Then, having altered his appearance slightly by removing his moustache and changing his style of coiffure, he presented himself to the *chetty* as the deceased's brother, armed with the letter, on which he levied heavy blackmail for the rest of his life, constantly threatening to ruin the *chetty's* business by an exposition of the dastardly inhumanity which drove a debtor to suicide.

Indications of the existence of a subterranean salt water channel beneath the Peninsula are not lacking. On 19th May, 1905, at Navaly, a small hole appeared in the ground, accompanied, according to local enthusiasm, by a loud, rumbling explosion, at which the earth split. The hole continued to enlarge into a pool, about forty feet deep, and salt, with its surface about two feet below ground-level. By a process of erosion the size of the pool is steadily increasing, to the extreme annoyance of the landowner, who has made numerous unsuccessful efforts to sell his unruly property.

The Jaffna cultivator has perfected the use of the well "sweep," or lever; he balances it so nicely that it needs but a slight pull or change of weight at the point of leverage to bring down the upraised point in order to lower the bucket into the well. When watering extensive gardens the "sweep" is worked by a man walking backwards and forwards on it, his change of position altering the balance, so that the point is raised and lowered automatically, while his wife empties the big basket-work bucket into a stone trough, which leads the water into an ingenious maze of channels.

His field or garden is a fitting environment wherein to leave the industrious Tamilian, whose national characteristics seldom fail to interest, and usually succeed in attracting the liking and respect of those who live long in the land of the Blind Minstrel.

CHAPTER ELEVEN

THE *PUNDIT'S* TALE

THERE lived in Jaffna a *pundit* of unrivalled sagacity and wit, whose instructional abilities were evidenced by a *chit*, received from a pupil known to be a competent judge: "Thambipillai has taught me Tamil against my inclination." He was a teacher of the old school, full of little songs, old-world maxims and often risky allusions, emphasizing his rules of grammar, while his syntax examples could not all have graced the pages of Dr. Pope.

Arriving punctually, and seating himself in his chair, his turban on the table and his rickety glasses on his nose, Thambipillai embarked upon the most intricate points of construction with a light heart and gravely merry phraseology, that left his pupil in spasms of laughter, sorry that the hour's grammar was over, instead of relieved at its expiration.

Like others, the *pundit* had his misfortunes, the most grievous being that his family increased while his salary remained the same. This accident, though viewed with humorous philosophy, coloured his life, conversation and profession, intruding itself both in English into Tamil and Tamil into English.

An actor of no mean histrionic power, the *pundit*, clad in a royal robe, with purple plush breeches and black stockings, seated upon a throne, was a kingly figure indeed, unrecognizable as the homely philosopher of the morning Tamil lessons.

This tale is his, whether he inherited or invented it. As told by him, with occasional snatches of song, breathing the essence of the East, in Tamil whose concentrated allusive meanings are not always translatable, it held his listeners in delighted amusement from beginning to end.

There was a King of Jaffna who had the marvellous gift of being able to transfer his soul into the body of a dead person and to return at will to his own body. He acquired this power during a trip to heaven—but that is another story. His Prime Minister, a very wise and experienced official, disapproved, with very good reason, of one of the King's friends, a crafty and unscrupulous "*tatchan*" (carpenter), called Tambian. Besides the fact that it was unseemly for the monarch to be on intimate terms with a carpenter—and withal a most rascally carpenter—the King had unwisely entrusted to Tambian the secret method whereby he effected the magical transitions of his soul.

However, notwithstanding the warnings of his Minister, the King one day went hunting alone with his friend. At mid-day they lay at rest beneath a tree, and the King, gazing up into the branches, saw a parrot sitting beside her dead mate. It occurred to the Royal brain that it would be interesting to be a "*kuli*" (parrot) for a short time, and he forthwith transferred his soul into the body of the dead bird, leaving his own lifeless body below the tree.

Then was the wisdom of the Prime Minister's warning borne out. Tambian, ever on the watch for such a chance as this, and only feigning sleep, quickly transferred his soul into the King's body, and, thinking it better to keep the King at a disadvantage for some time, buried his own body.

The King-Parrot, on his return from a short flight, finding himself compelled to remain a parrot for the present, determined to extract some amusement from the situation.

The carpenter-king meanwhile returned to the palace and proceeded to take full advantage of his Royal prerogatives, sampling the cellars and the kitchen to excess, but making signal lack of progress among the ladies, whose quick feminine intuition soon gathered that his uncouth manners were not those of their true King. The wise Prime Minister, too, though puzzled at first, quickly solved the mystery, realizing that he had to deal with the body of the King but the mind of the carpenter. The problem he yet had to elucidate was the identity and whereabouts of the Royal soul.

The King-Parrot in the meantime joined a large flock of parrots and rapidly, owing to his commanding character, became their leader. During a time when food was scarce a bird-catcher came into the jungle and, having fixed his net, spread grain upon the ground below it. The parrots saw the grain and began to circle down to it, when the "*Rasa-Kuli*" (King-Parrot) warned them that danger lay there. Notwithstanding his advice they descended to the generous display of food, and the King-Parrot perforce went with them. No sooner had they settled than down fell the net.

Then said all the parrots: "Indeed, O Rasa-Kuli, we were foolish not to listen to your wise words; now suggest a way out of this trap and we will all follow your instructions." The King-Parrot, with ready wit, bethought himself at once of a scheme.

"Presently," said he, "the bird-catcher will come to take us one by one out of the net and put us in a cage. We must all pretend to be dead, then he will throw us aside in a heap for eating purposes. There are one hundred of us here; the first parrot, as he falls, must count one, and continue to count up to a hundred as he hears each successive bird fall from the bird-catcher's hand. When he hears the hundredth bird fall he must shriek aloud, and we will all spring up and fly away."

It happened just as the King-Parrot said. The bird-catcher, in disgust, threw aside each apparently dead bird as he picked it out of the net, till only one was left—the King-Parrot. Just as the man stooped to pick up this last one his knife fell out of his waist on to the ground. The first parrot, thinking the thud was the fall of the hundredth parrot, shrieked, and the ninety-nine flew away, leaving the King-Parrot in the net.

The *Rasa-Kuli* was in imminent danger of being slain by the infuriated bird-catcher, but he said: "Oh, man, do not kill me, and, by my great gift of speech, I will make thee rich." Realizing that he had found a great prize the bird-catcher refrained from killing the King-Parrot, who told him to offer his wonderful talking bird for sale at one thousand rupees. So together they went down Chetty Street, the bird-catcher crying, "*Kuli! Kuli! Kuli!*" after the fashion of his trade. Many people asked the price of the fine parrot, who at once named his own figure, one thousand rupees; but the price was too high. At last a *chettiar* to whom one thousand rupees was nothing, seeing the King-Parrot's fine intelligence, gave the necessary sum and hung his purchase in a cage at the door of his shop.

Here the King-Parrot soon became a celebrity, crying the price of the wares and constantly giving tongue to wise and pithy epigrams, so that people deserted the courts and came to him for settlement of their disputes.

Now at that time there lived in Jaffna a dancing girl of great beauty, named Sunthary, who would dance only for those who deposited, in advance, one thousand rupees. One day her maid, while passing a well where two young men were bathing, overheard one tell the other that he had dreamt that he watched Sunthary dancing. The dancing girl, on hearing this from her maid, flew into a passion of rage, declaring that the young man must make good her fee of one thousand rupees. The youth refused to admit his liability, and the dancing girl and he agreed to go to the King-Parrot to have their case decided.

After hearing the arguments on both sides the King-Parrot, before a vast crowd of spectators, ordered a long pole, with one thousand rupees in a bag tied to the top, to be set up in the ground, and a large mirror placed at its foot. Then, calling the dancing girl, he bade her look in the mirror, with these words: "In like manner as this young man, by means of a vision in a dream, was a spectator of your dancing, so you, by means of a vision in the mirror, are the recipient of this thousand rupees, the fee you earned."

The public loudly applauded this ingenious judgment, but Sunthary was extremely annoyed, and abused the bird roundly, threatening him with vengeance for his adverse decision.

The *chettiar* to whom the King-Parrot belonged was a great friend of Sunthary, but at the time he was away in India, and did not hear of this *cause célèbre.* On his return, Sunthary would not see him until he brought her the King-Parrot, so the unfortunate bird, being unprotected by law in the exercise of his magisterial functions, was handed over to the enemy he had made in his judicial capacity.

The dancing girl gloated over her victory, keenly anticipating the pleasure of picking the delicate flesh from his bones. When she went out to worship at the temple and take an oil bath, she ordered her maid to kill him and cook him with extreme care. The maid opened the door of the cage, and, putting in her hand, was in the act of seizing the bird when he gave her a very sharp and vicious peck. Quickly she withdrew her hand, and as quickly out came the captive, flying away to safety. The maid was terrified, knowing how furious her mistress would be at the loss, when the King-Parrot, sitting in a near-by tree, said: "Kill a crow and cook it; your mistress won't know." The maid acted on this advice, and the dancing girl, in fine fettle after her bath, crunched the meat between her little teeth, revelling in the joy of eating the detested Parrot.

Now there was one thing the dancing girl feared, and that was death. Wherefore she constantly prayed to her sculptured deity that she might have everlasting life. One day, as she prayed, a voice proceeded from the image: "On the first day of the month of '*Sittirai*' (April) ride hither on an ass, and, before noon, a flaming chariot will descend and you will be carried living to an everlasting life in another sphere."

Sunthary was delighted, and, since the things she loved most were popularity and publicity, she asked the King and all his Court to see the great event. The expected miracle was of peculiar interest to the carpenter-king, since he, fearing the penalties he might suffer in the next world for his sins in this, also had a very lively desire to avoid death.

On the appointed day, in the presence of the entire Court, Sunthary arrived, looking very beautiful, but with her dignity slightly impaired by her lack of equestrienne skill upon an ass. Now the Prime Minister, having heard of the doings of the wonderful Parrot, had long suspected the truth of its identity, and was inclined to number the expected miracle among its escapades. He was, therefore, little surprised to hear a voice from the image proclaim that, as a punishment for Sunthary's love of pomp and extravagant show, the flaming chariot would not be coming that morning, and it was hoped that the public spectacle of her undignified seat upon the ass would be a useful lesson to curb her pride.

The crowd of guests rapidly dispersed, much amused by the dancer's downfall, while the

"WATCHED SUNTHARY CARRIED AWAY BY THE ASS."

King-Parrot flew from behind the image, and, perching on the shoulder of the Prime Minister, watched Sunthary, who had fainted from fury and shame, carried away by the ass, ignominiously and unattended.

The Minister, whispering to the King-Parrot that the kingdom was falling to pieces under the carpenter, warned him to be on the watch for an opportunity to regain his own body.

After this incident the Prime Minister spared no pains to create a situation favourable for his project of recovering the King. Circumstances soon came to his aid in the form of a deadlock between the carpenter-king and his harem. The ladies, loathing the vulgar character of the carpenter past endurance, locked themselves into the women's quarters. The rage of the false monarch satisfied them exceedingly, and he, in his dilemma, sought the advice of the wise Minister for the first time, feeling that feminine caprice was beyond his own ability to combat.

The Prime Minister, a favourite with the ladies, on account of his fine presence and ready wit, was already cognizant of this contretemps, and with subtle ingenuity had matured a solution fraught with favourable possibilities: He undertook to persuade the ladies, as, indeed, he had done already, to consent to a sporting event to decide whether they should continue to lock themselves into their rooms or not. The event was to consist of a fight between two rams, one representing the carpenter-king and the other the ladies.

If the King's ram won, the ladies were no longer to seclude themselves. If the harem ram won, the King was to provide himself with a fresh wifely complement.

The carpenter-king accepted the proposition, on the understanding that the Prime Minister should secure for him the finest available ram in the country. This proviso coincided well with that wise counsellor's plans, as the champion ram of the north had already been safely procured for the ladies, in anticipation of the event.

The harem ram, starting favourite on form and in public sentiment, finally killed the King's ram, after a bout of unexampled ferocity, but, before the fallen ram could be formally counted out, the carpenter, in desperation, transferred his soul to its lifeless body, and, springing up, it renewed the battle with unabated energy.

Here was the longed-for opportunity: a parrot fell dead from a neighbouring tree and the real King again took possession of his body, while the ladies' ram, fighting under the banner of beauty, killed its adversary a second time, inflicting terrible wounds. This was the end of the carpenter.

Rejoicing at the return of the ever-popular true King was universal; needless to say, the Prime Minister was raised to the peerage, and the victorious ram became a national hero, while the sentiments of the ladies, which can be well appreciated by all devoted wives, need no amplification.

CHAPTER TWELVE

THE ISLANDS

ALTHOUGH the name, "The Islands," is inevitably reminiscent of grass skirts, the soft wail of the ukelele and blue lagoons of the Pacific, there are, off the coasts of Jaffna, other islands, with no less charm and possibly even greater interest, where the ladies are equally alluring when young, the men far more industrious, and the lagoons just as blue.

The people are long-headed and canny—the Scotsmen of Jaffna—but cheerful and hardy, as befits a maritime race. As they are said to be backward and rustic, the name "*tival*" (islander) is used by the people of the mainland as a term of contempt, to which the islanders themselves object very strongly; in fact, its use frequently leads to a fight and a lawsuit, to whose intricacies all are devotedly attached. The standard of living is modest, so that the average man, unless he has lately had an expensive court case, is fairly well off; but it is most unlucky for him to name his worth—"perhaps Rs. 2000, perhaps Rs. 6000" is as near as he will specify, for fear disaster may visit him if he boasts of his wealth.

Lying in the fairway between Ceylon and India, "The Islands" were known in early times as ports of call to the Arab traders, whose books concerning their travels rejoiced in charming titles, such as *Meadows of Gold*, by Mas'udi. Among these books Rasanayagam Mudaliyar, to whom Jaffna is greatly indebted, conducted his researches, leading to the discovery of ancient references to this neighbourhood and the identification of places in the locality under long-forgotten names. In the thirteenth century El Edirisi wrote of a king called Jabeh, who ruled a number of islands, where ships took water on their way to China, probably on the west shore of Velanai Island, at a place now known as Chinan Kovil, where tradition has it that in olden times there was a Chinese settlement, whose buildings are now covered by the sandhills. Here, too, Labeh, King of Persia, chastised Bahu, the rebellious King of Ceylon, bringing with him for the purpose 16,000 war elephants and 2,000,000 soldiers in a vast fleet.

Marco Polo landed at a port in the north, probably Kayts, where "the people were idolaters, naked except for a cloth round the middle, ate flesh, drank tree wine and grew *sesamum* (*gingelly*)." In 1275 Kazwanai speaks of a sea-cow which suckled its young, evidently a dugong, caught in the sea of El Kulzam, which is said to be the area between North Ceylon and

India, while the heroes of the *Histoire de la Campaigne de Jesus*, in 1560, captured mermaids in the same sea and took them to Goa to be dissected. In 1272 John of Montecorvino records that as many as sixty vessels a year were wrecked on the islands in the northern passage between Ceylon and India. Although a number of these ships struck at Adam's Bridge, Delft and Nainativu took their toll, as indicated by the contemporary edict of Parakrama Bahu concerning wrecks, found engraved on a stone at Nainativu Temple.

The Dutch, who followed the Portuguese in the occupation of the district, were struck by the resemblance of the Jaffna Islands to their own home Archipelago; they therefore called them by their European names (given in brackets), following as nearly as they could the same geographical order. It will be noticed that, with the exception of Delft, all the Tamil names end in "tivu," which means island.

Punnalai causeway leads from the mainland to Karaitivu (Amsterdam), passing on the way Thorattapputti, a very small islet in the mouth of the lagoon, whose only importance is to indicate that this entrance to the lagoon has been too shallow for shipping for several hundred years, or on the islet would be found the remains of a fort. There is little doubt that all along the west coast of Karaitivu there have been, from very ancient times, small ports and landing places. Kayts is said to be the old port of Kala, described by historical writers, and is yet a large port, while quite near, on Karaitivu, is a place called Kalabhumi.

On the western shore of Karaitivu is a large mound full of the ruins of a building, which must have been of considerable size; it is known as Surian-piddy, the Tamil equivalent of Sunnyside, and is said to be haunted by its old occupants, probably Portuguese officers, who used the pleasantly situated house as a country residence. A Tamil palace may have stood on the spot before the Portuguese era, but without excavation it is impossible to say when the ruin originated.

Near the present jetty at Karaitivu West is the site of the Elephants' Quay, whence, Baldaeus says, "the elephants are embark'd by means of a bridg, and transported to Coromandel and Bengale." This is the original site of the port that shifted, in Dutch times, to the other side of the roadstead, called Kayts, a modification of the Portuguese Caes and Dutch Cays. The actual position of the Elephant's Quay is yet known by the exact Tamil equivalent Anai-palam, but it appears as if the whole strip of coast along the eastern side of Kayts harbour was known a century ago by this name.

Shipbuilding has always been an important industry in Kayts, and is still practised in the same manner as in olden times; numbers of "*dhonies*" (fishing-boats) are built yearly, but the schooner industry is confined to dry-docking and repairing. A deep channel is dug inshore on the Karaitivu side of the harbour, up which the schooner is floated, then the end of the channel is blocked and the water expelled by filling the "dock" with earth, which, banked up against her sides, serves also to keep the ship upright. Later, timber baulks and ropes are substituted and the earth is removed as required for repairs to the hull, the ship being raised, when necessary, by a simple leverage system and blocks inserted beneath her keel, which eventually arrives at ground-level. After the repairs are completed the ship is lowered and floated out of the dock at a suitable tide.

Kayts harbour, being the only port between Trincomalee and Rameswaram that is secure in all monsoons, is rich in defences. The Portuguese built a guard-house or small fort and established their customs on the Elephants' Quay, at the same time erecting a fort on the island at the mouth of the harbour, now called Hammenheil, and another on Velanai Island, known by the unaccountable name of Fort Eyrie.

There was in Portuguese times a fort known as the Fortaleza do Caes, a name that has been variously assigned to the original defences on Hammenheil and to Fort Eyrie, while the Portuguese foundations on the Caes itself have been overlooked. The land in which these ruins stand is called Rasaventotum (The Garden of the King), and can lay the best claim to be the ruins of the Fortaleza do Caes, built on the site of the historic palace of the Tamil King of the Islands, whose capital was at Karaitivu West, where he could easily take ship to the different parts of his maritime kingdom. Within a hundred yards are the walls of another Portuguese building, from its shape probably a large store or barracks. The Fortaleza do Caes was a two-storeyed building, thirty or forty yards square, with several small rooms on the ground floor, and a passage from the landward side through the middle to the sea-front, where was a ledge six feet wide at tide-level for the convenience of those landing from boats.

There is a persistent legend that buried treasure is hidden among these ruins, and, as all know in The Islands, before touching an old building in search of treasure the devil who guards it must be appeased by a human sacrifice. In 1924 the body of a woman was found under a culvert near the end of the causeway with her head cut off. The deed had been done elsewhere and the body brought and hidden under the road ; evidence led to the arrest of a young man, when it was discovered that Rasaventotum belonged to the accused, and that he had cleared a considerable portion of the foundations just at the time that the lady was decapitated. These facts comprised a strong indication that she had been the victim of the necessary sacrifice. The accused was eventually convicted of the crime.

In the sea, about five hundred yards from the south-west point of Karaitivu and in the mouth of the Jaffna lagoon, is a small islet, on which strategical position the Portuguese built a fort, called by them either Fortaleza Real or Fortaleza do Rio—*i.e.*, Fort Royal or the Fort of the River—and later named Hammenheil by the Dutch. In 1658 the Dutch captured this fortress after a fortnight's siege, vividly portrayed in Baldaeus' contemporary description of Ceylon :

"The better to straiten the Castle of Jafnapatam, and take away from the Garison all hopes of relief, it was thought necessary to attack a certain Outwork or Redoubt, built upon a small Isle in the middle of the River, not far from its Entrance, which it commands. This Fort was built by Anthonio, Amiral de Menezes, and may justly be call'd the Key of Jafnapatam. . . . Accordingly we detach'd a good Body of Men to the Isle of Ourature (Kayts), in order to attack the said Fort, in which, at that time, commanded one Hieronimo de Paiva with a good Garison. The Isle of Ourature (where formerly the Portuguese had a Castle (Fort Eyrie), the Ruins of which are yet to be seen), lying at some distance from this Water-Fort, we were forc'd to raise our Batteries against it upon the Isle of Caradiva : But finding that, by reason of the distance between us and them, and the strength of the Wall, we could make no breach in it, it was resolv'd to assault the place with Breastworks and Cannon. But before we thought fit to venture so desperate an Attempt, it was resolved to send the following Summons to the Commander of the Fort:

"'It having pleased Almighty God to bless our Arms with such success, that there is no possibility left for you to resist us, or defend yourself against our Attacks. It is, therefore, that we have thought fit to let you know (as is usual upon such occasions) that we are come to summon the Fort of Cays, in the name of the States-General of the United Provinces, . . . ; as by these Presents I summon the said Fort, not questioning but that after you have given sufficient Proofs of your Courage, you will now consider how unable you are to resist our Force. Don't therefore obstinately resist God's Will, and our Strength . . . in case you will be obstinate . . . we protest . . . that we are innocent of all the fatal Consequences and the Miseries that are likely to befall you . . . You have given sufficient Proofs of your Courage to admiration; it is time therefore you should now act with Prudence, and consult your safety. We expect your positive Answer within three hours by the Bearer of this. . . . Subscribing myself (as you think fit) either your Friend or Enemy.

"'The Admiral and General of the Dutch Forces, both by Sea and Land.

"'FROM THE CAMP,
10 *April*, 1658.'

"This letter, being translated into Portuguese, was sent into the Fort, the Commander whereof sent the following Answer:

"'That the Fort belonging to nobody, but to the King of Portugal his Master, he was oblig'd to maintain the same for his Majesty till the last drop of his Blood. That he could do no more than what pleased God to permit him, but neither he nor his Men were to be terrified by Threats.'

"This bold Answer made us think of nothing else but Force, so that we were preparing everything for an Assault, which would have cost us many a brave Fellow, had not the want of Fresh Water in the Fort oblig'd them to come to a Capitulation . . . They were glad to accept such Articles as we were willing to give them, which, however, were very honourable, the soldiers being allow'd to march out with all the Marks of Honour, and to be transported into Europe . . . The 28th of August I preach'd the Thanksgiving Sermon for this Surrender, upon the Text out of the 48th Psalm, ver. 8."

Ribeiro mentions the fort "at the entrance of the bar . . . next to that of the Ape" (Fort Eyrie), and also that "the enemy placed batteries on the point of the Caes dos Elefantes," but the wind and sandhills have obliterated all traces of the gun positions. Having taken Hammenheil, the Dutch demolished most of the old works and rebuilt them on their own model, the coral stone being passed from hand to hand by a chain of men, a yard apart, from Changanai, eight miles distant, with such speed that the walls were raised in six days. How the deeper water between the islet and Karaitivu was negotiated is not related by tradition; perhaps they used a bridge of boats. The name Hammenheil originated from the fact that the Dutch saw in the shape of Ceylon a strong resemblance to a ham, at whose heel stood this fort. It is a work, of fourteen angles, occupying the whole area of the island, with embrasured battlements and a fire-step for musketeers, while an unusually big gun must have been mounted towards the centre of the fort, on a large circular emplacement. The building is in a perfect state of repair, being used, when required, as an isolation hospital. The red roofs, austere coral walls rising from the sea, and stone jetty leading up to a gloomy portal form a picturesque setting to the historic fame of this isolated fortress.

On the island of Velanai (Leyden), covering the mouth of the harbour by a line of fire crossing that of Hammenheil, is the ruin of a Portuguese fort enveloped in mystery. The origin of its modern name of Fort Eyrie is quite unknown; the inhabitants of the locality call it Urundi (the place where the village was), but Eyrie has a European sound, quite incompatible with the associations of the neighbourhood, and appears to be the outcome of a visitor's mistake or whimsical nomenclature, perpetuated only on paper. The Portuguese name, "The Fort of the Ape," is suggestive of far more romantic, if not weird, theories as to its origin. It is conceivable that "the Ape" may have been an endearing term for some objectionable instrument of torture, kept ever-present in the mind of the populace by the name of the fortress that housed it. Penn, in *The Colombo Journal* of 27th February, 1832, said: "We have no way to ascertain when it was erected, most probably about 1669, it being thought necessary for the protection of the port, as well as to keep in awe the inhabitants of the Islands . . . It was a square of about 130 feet with four circular bastions, having walls of great thickness, and gateways in the east and west curtains. The sea washes the north face, the remains of a glacis are visible to the west, and the south face was protected by an outwork extending in a half-moon from bastion to bastion commanding the plain."

In the south-east corner of the "square" is a small chamber, part of whose vaulted roof is yet standing, evidently the chapel, for in the end wall is a niche intended for the Crucifix, the whole building well under cover of the fort wall. The outwork on the southern face contains living-rooms and is quite disconnected from the square; the passage between the two must, therefore, have been on an upper floor, a peculiarity noticeable in other Portuguese fortresses. The ruined walls are about twenty feet high, and in places ten feet in thickness.

Urathurai, the Tamil name of Kayts, is said to be derived from Ura-tota (Hog-ferry), the Sinhalese name of the place, so called because it is said that the god Sakra landed here after swimming over from India in the form of a pig. It is much more likely that it is a corruption of a Tamil name meaning "the place where the village guard is kept."

Kayts at the present day is famed for the excellent breakfasts prepared by the resthouse-keeper, Pillai, and his brother, but historically it boasts of being the site of the Dutch church of St. John and of the Customs House. In the resthouse compound is a large square tomb, with a conical top, on which is the pathetic inscription: "John, Infant Son of Robert Atherton, Esq. Died 23 Feb., 1828. Aged 3 Days." Robert Atherton was a commissioner of Jaffnapatam.

Not far away, in the police-station grounds, is another tombstone, erected to the memory of "Turbine: Died, July, 1913," an epitaph puzzling to those who do not know that it marks the grave of the faithful horse of a former Police Magistrate. Going further back in the magisterial line, when Kayts had a whole-time Magistrate of its own, there flourished a locally famous Tamil occupant of the Bench, who decided the innumerable petty quarrels of the people by placing complainant and accused opposite one another in court and telling them to carry on with their argument. He then heard both sides of the case at once, each side trying both vocally and logically to overcome the other; when he had heard enough to clear up the problem, or was in danger of being deafened, he decided in favour of the party whose vociferations were the more pithy and piercing. It is said that he was almost invariably right in his decisions.

On the west coast of Velanai is a celebrated ancient Mohammedan mosque, standing in a grove of trees a few yards from the sea-beach. Within its decrepit walls is a tomb regarded with great reverence. Many years ago a Tamil man was burying *olas* for manure when his *mamootie* struck the handsome corpse of a Moor, causing a wound which bled freely. This phenomenon puzzled him exceedingly, and that night the corpse came to him in a dream, saying that in life it had housed the soul of a saint, Abdul Abubakar, who now ordered him to go to the Lebbe in Jaffna and convey the wish of the deceased that a mosque should be built where the corpse was found, in order to venerate the place for ever. The mosque that the Lebbe built still stands, visited by Mohammedans, Hindus and Christians for its healing virtues. The tomb is a very long one, indicating that the saint was a big man; but it is not so much the sight of his resting-place as the air and water of the grove that draw the pilgrims.

Standing in a sheltered bay a peculiar eddy of the wind brings in a cool breeze off the sea during all monsoon, while the water of the well at the door of the mosque is of exceptional purity. As a consumptives' sanatorium it is remarkable; patients, who on arrival are revolted by the sight of food, are seen, after a three weeks' stay, eating heavy meals of rice and curry with relish. Very little money is spent on upkeep and repairs. Some time ago a ladder was needed to reach the courtyard lamp; next morning a ladder was washed up by the sea; in the same way a door frame was required and, after a high tide, one lay on the beach. No watcher is kept, because if anyone steals even a coconut from the grove he is first struck blind and drops the nut, and then bitten by one of the numerous cobras that live in the compound. In the event of doubt arising as to the accuracy of these facts, one need only ask in the neighbourhood for corroboration. An elderly Moor used to live near, called "The Hawk," because he never missed anything worth taking, who not only supported the details, but enlarged upon them; he was easy to find, being also a well-known legal tout.

Near the centre of the island is a ruin ascribed by local tradition to Alliarasani, a queen of olden time, but more likely to be Portuguese or Dutch, known as Kopparattadi (the Place of the Tower). It is now a mound of coral stones, with one corner wall showing up to about twenty feet, although the late Mr. J. P. Lewis was told in 1903 that a tower existed there "thirty years ago." Penn described it in *The Colombo Journal* of 6th January, 1832, as "A tower of fifty feet high and fifteen square, with walls of great thickness constructed with uncut coral. It cannot have been meant for defence; from the communication being external the rooms could hardly be intended for residence, although the upper was light and cool, but the terrace would be delightful in the cool of the evening, not only to invigorate the frame, exhausted by the heat of the day, but also for the view, which, extending over the adjacent country of lakes and islands from the fort at Kaits to Jaffna, would be wide and beautiful. It may have been intended for a signal post from the fort of Jaffna to those at Kaits."

Many years ago an Indian queen, named Alli, came to Allaipiddy in search of pearls; but something roused in her such affection for the place that she would not return to her native country; perhaps she married here, or she may have found the pearl-fishing so profitable that she would not leave it. Of the palace and temple that she built at Allaipiddy no ruins remain, but to the west of their site is a small lagoon, called Kappalladi (the place of the ships), where the queen's schooners anchored. Near the temple grew, so it is said, a Kotha tree, on a spot yet known as Kothamarattadi (The Place of the Kotha Tree), but no one knows what this tree looked like, although it appears to have been held very sacred. In Sinhalese "Kotha" means a Pinnacle.

In the temple always burned a light, whose position is now marked by a centuries-old ring of stones, inside which, at night, the temple lamp can still be seen burning, wherefore no one will live near. No one has ever seen it burning, but no one has ever dared to go and look. In 1922 Vinasy Philippan, while burying palmyrah fruit near the site of the palace, dug up a pot of unusual design, containing one hundred and seventy-nine gold Gujrati pagoda coins—a find which brought to light the fact that when the wind blows hard, and shifts the sand, old brass lamps, grinding-stones and other articles of great antiquity are found; while in 1877 a chain of gold coins was dug up in a depression where stand the ruins of a very old building. When the owner was deepening a Portuguese well near the Portuguese church he found, below the level originally sunk, a bronze bowl with lid, probably Indian, and of immense age. All these finds point to the truth of the legendary splendour of Allaipiddy, but, so the inhabitants say, the sand has since blown over from India and covered the fertile land and marks of former greatness. The people in old times were of huge stature, and lived to a great age; now, among the barren, scorching sand dunes, they are weaklings and die young. The sand is blamed for this—it has, they say, crushed their spirit.

Mandaitivu (included in Leyden) is undistinguished historically, but has a noteworthy type of inhabitants, characterized physically by a very small face surmounted by an extremely high forehead and domed head—a feature peculiar to Mandaitivu families. Between Mandaitivu and Jaffna is a low islet covered with scrub, called Sirutivu (the small island), where, before attacking Jaffna, the Portuguese army erected an altar, and after Mass had been celebrated, listened to a sermon exhorting them to extend the realms of Christianity by conquering the Jaffnese. In later times this island was used as an isolation camp, probably when Mandaitivu and Velanai were desolated by the small-pox in 1884, so that it is still marked on old maps as Small-pox Island, and known by that name to old Jaffna residents.

The other tiny islands of the lagoon have little to recommend them except partridge shooting, although, in May, Mántivu presents a striking appearance, being covered with giant thistle-downs, a foot and more in diameter, called in Tamil "*mooli*," which roll and bounce along the ground at a great pace when stirred by the wind. Down the coast are two islands, Hoorn and Enchuyfen, which, as recently as 1840, were known as "The Two Brothers," but are now called Iranaitivu. Here are the horse plains, where horses which were awaiting export were sent from the Government stud in Delft.

Parts of these islands are said to be haunted by ghostly visitants from the sea—possibly mermaids; the inhabitants speak of strange noises heard at night, but the nature of the noises does not appear to be definite enough to admit of explanation. It is a strange fact that at one season of the year all the numerous partridges migrate from Iranaitivu to the mainland and not one can be found on the two islands. In the open sea off Kalmunai is Palaitivu (Galue), where there is a Roman Catholic shrine, visited by hundreds of pilgrims in March and April, while farther out to sea lies Kakeraitivu (Calienye), entirely uninhabited.

Between Punkudutivu (Middleberg) and Velanai is the little island of Kanantivu, where, every evening in February and March, vast flocks of white cranes come to roost, covering the low shrubs and trees and filling the air with their cries. The only reason that presents itself for their predilection for the island is that it is uninhabited and quiet, but not far distant from their feeding grounds in the paddy-fields of the larger islands. Punkudutivu is large and populous, but devoid of historical or legendary interest, except for the story of some old buildings that once stood there, but have now been demolished and the stones used for their owners' houses.

Starting afresh on the outer chain of islands, Eluvativu, the Portuguese "Ilha Deserta," takes first place. It offers no object of peculiar interest, being more or less barren, as its name implies, but near to it lies Parattivu, an islet which gets its name from the enterprise of a gentleman named Mr. Muttiahpillai, who cultivated cotton there; the plant grew well, but, owing to the expense and difficulty of transport, the profit was not commensurate with the expenditure and he gave up the venture, leaving, to perpetuate its memory, only the name Cotton Island, where a few plants still flourish.

South of Parattivu is Analaitivu (Rotterdam), where are the ruins of a building mentioned by Baldaeus, who also remarks that it produces a vast quantity of "Oisters." "It has a little Church and convenient house near it. It was formerly call'd Donna Clara, from a certain lady that liv'd there, and was mistress of it in the time of the Portuguese. They still show there a chair, wherein she used to sit, which is big enough to hold conveniently two Persons at once."

Separated by a very narrow channel is a tiny islet, conspicuous only for the tamarind-tree of immense size that gives it the name of Puliantivu.

The southern island of the chain, separated from Punkudutivu by a channel two miles wide, is Nainativu (Haarlem), so called, Baldaeus says, because of the number of jackals to be found there. Here, in a forgotten age, the Sinhalese built a Buddhist temple, at a place still called Buddha Kovil, where the foundation of a square-walled enclosure that surrounded a Bo tree is visible, while the cut stones of the *vihare* lie scattered about the neighbourhood. Although the Buddhist remains can claim priority in the matter of antiquity, the most conspicuous feature of the island is an ancient Hindu Nagammal temple, to which flock hundreds of pilgrims yearly. It is an imposing structure, built at the centre of the island, on the shore of the channel, with a considerable stone jetty at which the boatloads of pilgrims can land. The figure of the deity within is seated on the coils of a five-headed cobra, whose heads come up from behind and spread out like a canopy, protecting the head of the seated deity. On the steps of the shrine are two inscribed stones, but no one knows what is written on them; they are covered and stained with the oil and deposit of hundreds of years' offerings to the deity enshrined within.

In the temple compound is a large tablet of stone, inscribed on both sides. On one side the inscription is in a language mainly the same as modern Tamil, but the other side is at present unread with any accuracy. The readable side proclaims that elephants were exported *via* Nainativu to India, and that at this spot mendicants and shipwrecked people received alms and food from the proceeds of a tax levied upon the cargo of every ship that called there.

In the sea, off the north point of Nainativu, about half-a-mile from the temple, are two large coral rocks three hundred yards apart. On the western one is said to be carved a cobra, while the eastern is believed to bear the impress of the footprints of a big bird. The western rock is shaped like an hour-glass, and the other is supposed to resemble a bird's head, but the likeness is too faint to be seen from any angle, even when the creature's features are pointed out by an imaginative islander. On the hour-glass rock there is no trace of any marking whatever, so that the investigator is ill-advised to visit these curiosities, as a knee-deep paddle is involved over very sharp prickly coral for a quarter of a mile.

There is a story about these two rocks from which, according to local tradition, the worship of the cobra at this ancient temple originates. A very rich merchant was sailing from India to Ceylon, and when he arrived off the north-west coast of Nainativu he saw a cobra coiled round the western rock. It lay round the "waist" of the "hour-glass." On the eastern rock sat a bird called a Brahminy kite, which can cure snake-bites by a look, and at sight of which all snakes hide. The bird was going to kill the cobra, but the merchant, feeling compassion for the snake, asked the bird not to kill it, and offered a great sum of riches in support of his request. The bird accepted the present and allowed the cobra to go unharmed.

The merchant returned to his Indian home after the most successful trading trip of his career, and, in addition to wealth acquired in the course of business, he found on his finger a ring of incalculable value. His wife, although welcoming his triumphal return, was, one would think, unduly suspicious concerning the acquisition of the ring, and had a secret objection to the fact that the cobra had taken up its residence in her house. She communicated her trouble privately to her husband, who then displayed a marvellous example of marital acquiescence. He pondered over a solution of the problem of dispensing with the cobra's presence without causing offence, also over the ring matter, and at length again set sail for Ceylon, filled with a great purpose. He landed at the spot where he had saved the cobra from death, on Nainativu, and there founded a temple dedicated to the worship of the cobra, and gave the ring to the temple. On his return home he found his wife's suspicions allayed, and the cobra departed, leaving in its place a further huge pile of jewels and rare wealth.

Seven miles out at sea, to the south-west of Nainativu, lies the island of Delft, where the imagination is irresistibly drawn to the arresting figure of Nolan, an Irish horse-breeder, who filled the island with his powerful personality during the early half of last century. It would, however, be a waste of interesting anecdote not to touch first, in more or less chronological order, upon the traditions of the earlier races who controlled Delft before the arrival of the

British. The legendary first inhabitants were, as in the rest of Ceylon, beings of huge stature, called Nagas. After them apparently came a few Sinhalese, who built a *dagoba* and a temple at the north-east end of the island, usually known as Vadiresan's Fort, but of them there is no tradition.

The departure of the Sinhalese seems to have been caused by the incoming of the Mukwars from Coromandel.

Vadiresan was their king, who left his name in Delft; he built a fort somewhere in the island, probably on the site subsequently used by the Portuguese for the same purpose, but certainly not at the place which popular tradition assigns to him, where the mound of earth and brick, surrounded by a litter of worked stones, marks the position of the *dagoba* mentioned above. He is said, too, to have been the original constructor of a canal which runs across Delft, connecting two large tanks. The canal is now only about twenty feet wide, and very shallow; Vadiresan may have been the first to dig the channel, but it has been certainly improved and repaired in comparatively recent years.

The Mukwars evidently used Delft as a stepping-stone to northern Ceylon. The nobility and knights of the invading host, having determined on a descent upon the mainland, set off in a boat, attended by a small force. Just before entering the narrow seas between Nainativu and Punkudutivu they came to a meeting of a number of currents, where the sea is always rough, even on the calmest day. The Mukwar knights struck this spot on a very rough day, their boat capsized, and all were drowned. Later, their ladies confident in the strength of their lords, followed, and having successfully weathered the passage, landed on the Jaffna mainland, fondly expecting the caresses of their victorious husbands. Instead, to their dismay, they were met by those of the inhabitants, delighted at such an unexpected windfall. Historians apparently deem it unnecessary to record more of this adventure.

The Mukwars eventually established themselves on the mainland—where some still exist—but in later years the Tamil people, having driven out most of them to the south-east, determined upon the conquest of Delft. With this purpose in view a Tamil fleet sailed for Delft and met the Mukwar fleet off the north-west coast of Nainativu. After a fierce battle the Mukwars were defeated, and the Tamils, having conquered Delft, took it under their administration. At this juncture we enter upon comparatively recent historical times. The Tamil king sent one of his ministers, with his retinue, to look after Delft; this minister's name was Tannanayagam Mudali, and his retinue were the forefathers of the present inhabitants of the island. The peculiar conditions entailed by the close association of all castes in this enforced exile resulted in relaxations of some of the usual caste prohibitions in various directions, evidence of which can be daily seen in the habits of the people and relations between the castes at the present day. All castes climb trees in order to procure their staple nourishment, *toddy*—a practice unthought of, except with horror, by *vellalas* on the mainland. The site of Tannanayagam Mudali's residency is still in the hands of his direct descendant, the ex-Police Vidhan, of Delft West, who retired owing to old age, and the foundations of the buildings were removed only about thirty years ago, in order to bring more land under cultivation.

Traces of the Portuguese administration of Delft remain in the ruins of a fort which was undoubtedly built by them, as Dutch military architecture was of a more modern type. It is a very strongly fortified two-storeyed dwelling, covering an area about fifty yards square, with a double centre wall of immense thickness. This wall completely cuts the fort in half at ground-level, the only means of communication being on the first floor—a common precautionary measure in defensive structures of that period. As a result, it is a very complicated edifice, full of long narrow and little square rooms.

The stairs run in the double walls, and lead out on to what must have been a flat roof, judging from the marks of the rafter sockets in the masonry. In one corner is the dungeon, a small square room, with a floor below ground level, without any door, and having only one small window about two feet square, leading into the interior of the fort. The unfortunate prisoners must have been pushed in through this little aperture, or let down through a trapdoor in the floor above, and could have got out only by means of a rope; a good many must have met their death in this little chamber.

There is one large room which has the appearance of a mess-room, and a large number of small sleeping-rooms connected by corridors.

The Dutch built a barracks about a quarter of a mile from the fort, and within their premises is a fine large Residency, now in use as the Government bungalow. The barracks were surrounded by a wall, a great part of which still stands, enclosing an area of about two hundred square yards. One of the barrack rooms is still in existence, although part of the wall has fallen almost to ground level. The most striking building is the Dutch dovecot, still in a state of perfect repair. It is made of coral stone, with a solid base about eight feet square, up to a height of fifteen feet, surmounted by a stone pigeon-house of five storeys of the same floor space, and rising to a height of thirty feet at the apex of the roof. There are numbers of little doorways, and accommodation for hundreds of pigeons, but, although the "*maniagar*" (chief headman) has once or twice put pigeons in, and fed them carefully, they will not stay, in spite of every encouragement. The present Village Tribunal Court, in which is hung a portrait of Sir William Twynam, who took a great interest in the island, stands within the limits of the barracks.

The Delft people divide their land into "*seemals*" (enclosures), by means of stone walls, such as are built in Ireland and the West of England. Paddy will not grow with any success, and live stock, particularly sheep and goats, are the main agricultural interest. On account of the numbers of stray animals, all straw- or hay-stacks have to be built on platforms five or six feet from the ground. These platforms are made by lashing poles from two adjacent palmyrah-trees, to a tulip-tree, planted for the purpose of forming the apex of the triangular platform, or to two tulip-trees, completing a square platform.

Delft is noted for longevity; one old lady actually reached the age of one hundred and sixty, while another, named Sinnachchi, lived to be a hundred, and Kunchchi, also of the weaker sex, was full of life and talk at one hundred and ten. Kunchchi regarded the present generation as decadent, and not to be compared with the young people of her time. Sinnachchi looked her age; she was shrivelled and unable to rise from a squatting posture, but until within two years of the end of her life she went annually to Jaffna to see her relations who lived there. The people put down their length of days to good milk, palmyrah *odial*, sea-air, no worries, and innocence of heart. These seem to be excellent causes. *Toddy*, one notices, is not included. It forms the staple diet of all the poorer classes, but whether it assists length of life, or is the counteracting influence that prevents everyone in Delft from living to be about two hundred, it is impossible to say.

On going a farther ten miles out to sea there is a small island called Kachchativu, on which is said to grow, in addition to numerous other health-giving herbs, a kind of golden-coloured mistletoe, which, when eaten, gives immortal life. The mistletoe seems to be difficult to find, as even Delft people, up to date, have all gone the same way eventually. Unfortunately there is no water on Kachchativu, so no one lives there, but it is quite fertile. There is a small Roman Catholic shrine, and yearly, in March, about six hundred pilgrims visit it, occasionally meeting with considerable adversity while awaiting a favourable wind to return.

Among the many romantic figures of various nationalities who have drawn more or less attention to their careers in Ceylon, one of the most attractive is Lieutenant Nolan, of the 4th Ceylon Regiment, who, for thirteen or fourteen years, reigned over Delft after the fashion of an old-time raja. A man of outstanding character, and decided ability, he has left behind him in that small island a crop of traditions and stories, based on fact, which will perpetuate his memory to posterity as a figure of heroic proportions.

Although there still existed in 1924 a few old people who remembered him, most of the incidents of his career are now recited in a spirit of half-belief, as tales told to children, and anecdotes deriving their humour from their somewhat risky flavour. Fortunately Kunchchi —who has been mentioned on the previous page—remembered him well in her youth, and certainly her description shows that he was one who might well be expected to have impressed his features upon the feminine mind. He was "Very big, broad, and tall, with brown hair, grey eyes, a skin as white as milk, and he looked at you in such a way that women all ran away when they saw him coming." Besides this, he always wore a black top-hat, and was an Irishman. The old lady's description contained such fervour that it suggested the possibility of a long-buried romance, but tact forbade further inquiry. From local gossip it appears that the Lieutenant, besides being a first-rate agriculturist, judge, administrator and horse-breeder, also combined the appearance of an Adonis with the propensities of Don Juan and King Solomon.

In July, 1811, when Thomas Eden, Esquire, was Collector of Jaffnapatam, the Right Honourable John Wilson, Lieutenant-Governor and Commander-in-Chief in and over the

British Settlements in the Island of Ceylon in the Indian Seas, appointed Lieutenant Edward tedlan to proceed to the island of Delft "for the purpose of making experiments of the soil and of the general practicability of improving the cultivation of Flax in this Island and for dressing it in the European manner and manufacturing it into Canvas." Mr. Thomas Eden was instructed "to afford Lieutenant Nolan every assistance in his power without incurring any public expense." The scheme was evidently intended to provide tenting and cordage for the army and fleet in Ceylon, and, contrary to the current idea, Nolan was not sent to look after, or start, a stud of horses in Delft. The horses were already there, under the control of the Collector of Jaffnapatam, who even then exported a considerable number. After his arrival in Delft, Nolan devoted himself to flax, and exported large consignments to Ceylon, which were usually taken to Trincomalee to make cordage. He had some difficulty over money, as there appears to have been none in the island; then the Government sent him some, but it was nearly all large notes, and as there was no small change he was scarcely better off. The industry grew, and in July, 1812, he required a large labour force; to begin with he procured labour under Government authority, and "impressed" men. At this juncture he was sternly told that as the flax enterprise was entirely his private concern he must not commandeer labour under Government auspices, while the Collector of Jaffnapatam was instructed to see that he did not do so.

On 20th February, 1812, one Mr. Sansoni was appointed to the office of Superintendent of the Stud at Delft, on a salary of 390 rix-dollars, 4 fanams and 2 pice *per mensem*, but in July, " The Governor having under his consideration the state of the Public Expenditure, as compared with the amount of Revenue of this Island, is forcibly impressed with the necessity of having recourse to every practicable means which can in their effects be productive of economy, his attention has, in consequence, been directed to the situation held by Mr. Sansoni of Superintendent of the Stud at Delft . . . and not being able to comprehend how that establishment can be benefited by the superintendence of a person resident at this place, desires that you (the Collector of Jaffnapatam) will be so obliging as to inform him of the manner in which the Stud has been managed in the past." The axe fell, and poor Mr. Sansoni lost his job. From then onwards Nolan looked after the stud, under the control of the Collector, and brought it to a state of wonderful perfection. He was called " Superintendent of the Island of Delft," and dealt with judicial, customs, and all administrative duties with great efficiency.

The horses of which Nolan took charge were the Government stud, descended from those introduced into Delft by the Portuguese; so

NOOSING WILD HORSES IN DELFT
(This picture is a copy of an illustration in the Reverend Baldaeus' *Account of Ceylon*)

the Rev. Baldaeus, in his book dated 1671, tells us, wherein also, having described how the horses were caught by driving them into swamps, then noosing them, he relates that they were small and wiry, and excellent at going over stony places: a very accurate description.

In Nolan's time two Persian stallions and one or two Arabs from Negapatam were brought into the stud, which increased into a really big concern. The main stock of the horses ran wild on the vast Horse Plains which cover the south-western side of the island, but Nolan built three sets of stables, in Delft East, Centre and West. The stables in Delft West, which seem to have been intended for the horses in the first stage of their training, are of great size and length; two long, connected buildings, each to contain thirty or forty horses, with sixty pillars, stretching for one hundred and fifty yards, and one dividing wall in the middle. Near these stables are sixty wells sunk in the coral rock, some of them to a great depth, and all connected by a maze of coral-built channels and aqueducts, giving water accommodation for hundreds of horses at one time.

The stables in Delft Centre are of the same type, but smaller, with only thirty pillars, and were probably used for trained animals; the site of those in Delft East, although they have now disappeared, is still called the "training stables," Evidently the "school" was situated here. Many of the trained colts were shipped over to the twin islands of Iranaitivu, whence they could be easily sent to the mainland as required, at any time of year. The stud was maintained after Nolan left, but was given up about 1870, when Government found that it no longer paid. Thirty or forty horses still run wild on the horse plains, fine, strong little animals that might well repay careful training.

From 1813 until about 1819 Nolan, who probably taught the Delft people to build the Irish stone walls which surround their fields, ruled Delft with an iron hand, exporting horses all over Ceylon, and even to India. He lived in the present Government bungalow, which in former times was the Residency of the Dutch Governor, where he held Court, established his *kachcheri*, and, for a bachelor, maintained an unusually large household. Far from being averse to feminine society, he has the reputation of comparing on equal terms with the Sultan Schariah of *Arabian Nights* fame. The grounds of the Residency formed a pleasuance worthy of any Eastern potentate, where, beneath the shade of luxurious palms, hundreds of doves cooed slumberously, housed in the Dutch stone dovecot. He was an amiable and paternal despot, who looked well after the health of his subjects; when there was a famine he fed them at his own expense, from great cauldrons at the stables in Delft Centre. Within easy distance of the Residency a canal was cut, connecting the sea with the two large tanks in the interior, between which was Vadiresan's channel and continuing right through to the opposite coast. Here Nolan had a boat made of leather, in which he paddled himself down the canal to the stables and horse plains; but he had also a pleasure punt, in which, on Sunday evenings, he caused himself to be poled quietly over the pleasant waters, as he whiled away the fleeting hours with the youthful beauties of Delft.

A great number of Delft people have grey eyes—"Footprints on the sands of Time."

The canal, although rather silted, is still navigable; it is said that the introduction of salt water by its means into the tanks in the interior has caused Delft to be very much more arid then it used to be.

It was when he was at the summit of his career that those who objected to some of Nolan's actions, headed by the Maniagar, took advantage of his weaknesses, and built them up into a formidable charge, which they embodied in a petition to Government, signed by thirty-eight people. The Petition charged him with having used his authority as a Government servant to increase his harem, by refusing process in judicial proceedings unless the desired lady was brought, besides inflicting stripes in default of her production; causing a girl to hang herself; misappropriating a valuable bond filed in a case; and oppressing people of all classes. His Excellency, upon receiving it, referred it to a commission, composed of W. H. Hooper, Esq., Collector, and Chas. Scott, Esq., Provincial Judge of Jaffnapatam, for inquiry. The inqury was held at great length on the island of Punkudutivu. The evidence in support of the Petition was poor, the actual incidents complained of all happened a year or two before the Petition was written, and most of the signatories denied their signatures, or said that they merely signed under compulsion. Almost all the prosecution witnesses said they had no complaint at all against Nolan. The ladies in question did not appear, although it is nowhere alleged that there was anything to prevent them from doing so. Nolan's defence was that in the proper performance of his duties as a Magistrate he had "become obnoxious" to the headmen. The commissioners, as the petitioners could not prove their case, saw no reason to disbelieve him, and he was acquitted. Nolan then charged the petitioners with conspiracy, and a fresh inquiry was held before the same commissioners. During the trial Nolan asked for most of the accused to be discharged, as he verily believed on his oath that they had been led astray, signing his request:

Eventually the six leaders were committed, on

their admission of guilt, to the Supreme Court.

There is no doubt that Nolan carried out his duties well, and did not abuse his power; he nowhere denies his numerous amours, but he makes it clear that they were a thing apart from his office. It must have been evident, however, to the Government, that his Oriental habits were sapping his efficiency as Superintendent of Delft, and, in 1824, he took his pension in a lump sum and retired to his home in Ireland, where he died some twenty years later, leaving a name distinguished above many others in the East.

DATES

Landing of Wijaya in Ceylon .	543	B.C.
Buddhism introduced into Ceylon .	307	,,
Earliest Tamil Invasion . .	237	,,
Elara slain by Duttha Gamini .	161	,,
Sinhalese Kings rule Ceylon, with frequent periods of internal strife and occasional extension of Tamil power	160 B.C.-A.D. 1500	
The Portuguese Invasion . .	1517	A.D.
The Dutch Invasion . . .	1650	,,
The British Occupation .	1795	,,

GLOSSARY

Adigar. Ad-i-gar. The Kandyan chieftain of highest rank.

Aiyo! I-yo. Alas!

Anicut. An-i-cut. A dam across a stream directing water into paddy-fields.

Arachchi. Ar-ratchi. A minor headman, usually of a village, but also used as a title for other small posts.

Areca. Ar-ee-ka. A small tree of the palm family, which produces quantities of nuts used for chewing with the betel leaf.

Arrack. Pronounced as spelt. An intoxicating liquor distilled from *toddy*, the juice of the palm flower.

Bemma. As spelt. A rampart, terrace or sunk fence.

Betel-chew. Beetel. Sliced areca-nut and lime, folded in the leaf of a betel creeper for chewing purposes. Very astringent, but extensively used. The creeper is somewhat like a pepper vine.

Cabook. Ka-book. A hard red soil, solidified like brick, excellent for building purposes.

Cadjan. Kad-jan. The half of a cocon't branch, with the fronds woven like a mat. Used one above the other these make good fences.

Chena. Chay-na. A piece of land on a hill-side where low jungle growth has been burnt off to grow vegetables or hill-paddy. A fresh piece is used each year, as after a crop the ground must be left fallow for eight or ten years. The Sinhalese word is "*hena*."

C.L.I. Ceylon Light Infantry.

Dagoba. Dar-go-ba. A solid bell-shaped edifice of bricks, erected as a devotional monument to Buddha. Some are of gigantic size.

Dewale. Day-wa-le. A Buddhist temple where Hindu deities have a place of worship. Dewales were instituted when Hindu Royalty was brought from India to rule in Ceylon.

Durutu. Doo-roo-too. Spring.

Ela. El-a. Stream.

Fortaleza. Fort-ar-lay-za. Fortresses (Portuguese).

Ganga. Gun-ga. River.

Gansabhawa. Gun-sab-bar-wa. Village committee.

Gingelly. Jin-jelly. Sesamum. See under *Sesamum*.

Govinda. Go-win-da. An auspicious Tamil name for a deity, which is also used as an ejaculation of praise.

Guru. Goo-roo. Teacher.

Gurunanse. Goo-roo-nancy. Polite form of "guru."

Hoo-cry. The distance a man shouting "Hoo" can be heard.

Hoppers. Arpers. Pancakes, thick in the centre and thin round the edges, made of rice-flour.

H'ro! H'ra! Not satisfactorily translatable. An auspicious Tamil ejaculation of praise.

Lebbe. Leb-by. Mohammedan priest.

Mahavansa. Mar-ha-wan-sa. An ancient chronicle of Buddhism, in which is included much Ceylon history.

Maligawa. Mar-li-gar-wa. Palace.

Odial. O-di-yal A preparation made from the palmyrah fruit.

Ola. O-la. Leaf of a palm-tree.

Oya. Oi-ya. Stream.

Palmyrah. Pal-mire-ra. A tall tree of the palm family, with fan-shaped leaves and small round fruit. The bole is very dark coloured and there are no leaves or branches except at the very top.

Pansala. Pan-sa-la. Priests' residence at a Buddhist Temple.

Pundit. Pun-dit. Teacher.

Putha. Poo-ta. Son.

Ratemahatmaya. Ra-tay-mar-hart-may-ya. Kandyan chief or chief headman of a district.

Sadhu. Sar-doo. Alleluia.

Samanera. Sam-an-eer-a. Priest.

Sannas. San-nas. A copper engraved document, usually a title deed ; the term is also applied to similarly engraved stones.

Sesamum. Ses-a-mum. An annual grain with oily seeds.

Sri Pada. Sree Pad-a. The Holy Footprint on Adam's Peak.

Tat. A window-screen or sun-blind, usually made of long horizontal strips of bamboo, connected with string. It is rolled up by means of pulleys when not in use.

Tenna. Ten-na. Plateau of open grass-land.

Toddy. Tod-dy. The juice of the palm flower, which, when fermented, is intoxicating. It may be drunk sweet or fermented, and, like beer or milk, is both food and drink.

Vederala. Ved-er-a-la. A physician who practises Ayurvedic or Eastern theories of medicine.

Vidane. Ve-da-nay. The minor headman in charge of a village. The term is used in Tamil districts and some other parts of Ceylon to correspond with *arachchi.* There is also a "*vel-vidane*" in charge of paddy-land irrigation channels.

Vihare. We-har-ee. Room where image is kept at a Buddhist Temple.

Yaya. Yai-yar. A stretch of adjoining paddy-fields.

INDEX